THE ART & CRAFT OF
STONEWORK

The Art & Craft of
STONEWORK

DRY-STACKING MORTARING PAVING CARVING GARDENSCAPING

DAVID REED

LARK BOOKS

A Division of Sterling Publishing Co., Inc.
New York

&

To my parents,
Philip & Ann

Editor: JOE RHATIGAN
Art Director: CELIA NARANJO
Principal Photographer: DAVID REED
Cover Design: BARBARA ZARETSKY
Illustrations: DENISE DRUMMOND
Editorial Assistance: RAIN NEWCOMB and VERONIKA ALICE GUNTER

Library of Congress Cataloging-in-Publication Data

Reed, David.
   The art and craft of stonework : dry-stacking, mortaring, paving, carving, gardenscaping / by David Reed.
   p. Cm.
   Includes index.
   ISBN 1-57990-520-x
   1. Stonemasonry. I. Title

TH 5411 .R43 2002
693'.1—dc21

2001041745

10 9 8 7 6 5 4 3 2

Published by Lark Books, a division of
Sterling Publishing Co., Inc.
387 Park Avenue South, New York, N.Y. 10016

First Paperback Edition 2003
© 2002, David Reed

Distributed in Canada by Sterling Publishing,
c/o Canadian Manda Group, One Atlantic Ave., Suite 105
Toronto, Ontario, Canada M6K 3E7

Distributed in the U.K. by Guild of Master Craftsman Publications Ltd.
Castle Place, 166 High Street, Lewes, East Sussex, England BN7 1XU
Tel: (+ 44) 1273 477374, Fax: (+ 44) 1273 478606
Email: pubs@thegmcgroup.com, Web: www.gmcpublications.com

Distributed in Australia by Capricorn Link (Australia) Pty Ltd.
P.O. Box 704, Windsor, NSW 2756 Australia

If you have questions or comments about this book, please contact:
Lark Books
67 Broadway
Asheville, NC 28801
(828) 253-0467

Manufactured in China

ISBN 1-57990-520-x

CONTENTS

INTRODUCTION

AROUND THE WORLD AND THROUGHOUT HISTORY, stone has influenced and fascinated civilizations like no other building material. From the first primitive stone tools, dating back 2.5 million years, to the ancient stone circles used to mark time, from the classic towering stone cathedrals and castles to postmodern stone sculptures, stone has sparked the imagination of inventors, visionaries, artists, and craftspeople. Why? For one reason, because it's there. Stone is a readily found material, which probably inspired the first cave dweller to pick one up and smash it over a stubborn nutshell. Plus, stone is strong, sturdy, and, well, permanent.

But there's something else about stone—something a little less tangible that draws us to build and work with it even in this digital age. Perhaps it's the ancient story each stone has hidden within that creates an almost spiritual association, or it could simply be a way to reconnect with the earth. Maybe it's the primal satisfaction of toiling with stone and completing a project that's the perfect marriage of function and beauty (a way of combating our propensity toward instant gratification). Or, perhaps this satisfaction stems from building something well that will outlast you—something that speaks of great effort.

I've written this book to celebrate natural stone in all of its versatility. It may sound strange to hear someone talk of stone as being versatile, but after working with stone for more than 15 years, I can tell you that stone

A Nepalese woman travels this well-worn stone path through Marpha, located along the Annapurna Circuit in the Himalayan Mountains.

has an aesthetic appeal that has the ability to draw us closer to nature. It's also an extremely expressive building and decorating material with its variety of colors, shapes, sizes, and textures, that not only endures, but actually gets more beautiful as time passes. When you work with stone, you're building for the ages.

This book introduces you to many of the ways to build and decorate with stone. Whether you're thinking of building a wall, redesigning a garden, or simply seeking a new medium to express yourself, I'll take you through what you need to know to get started on your journey. Enjoy!

The remains of a stone barn built in the mid 1700s still stand in Hunderton County, New Jersey. The air vents worked into the gabled end are a unique feature.

Krishna's Butter Ball Stone, located in the town of Mamallapuram, India.

7

Chapter 1

ALL ABOUT STONE
A STONEMASON'S PRIMER

Pick up a stone. Feel it in your hand. What kind of stone is it? Where did it come from? How did it end up here in your hand? Some of the most interesting aspects of stonework include the variety of rocks available and their many attributes, and the language that has developed around this notion of using stone to build. This chapter will not only familiarize you with the language of stonework, but also describe the characteristics and qualities to look for in stones, and where and how to find the stones for your project. Sometimes it's as easy as picking out stones from a pile at the stone yard. Other times, you may have to search around a bit. Either way, don't under-estimate the creativity and joy involved in the hunt for the perfect stone.

STONES TO KNOW

THOUGH YOU PROBABLY HAD TO MEMORIZE the three main types of rocks in school, chances are you don't remember how they're different from one another. Igneous rock is extremely dense and hard (examples are granite and basalt). Sedimentary rock, such as limestone and sandstone, is of medium-density and is relatively easy to work with. Metamorphic rock includes any kind of stone that has been transformed by heat, pressure, or chemical action into another type of stone, such as marble, which is altered limestone, or gneiss, which was once granite. Within these categories are many kinds of rock with names that may vary from one region to the next.

Though not a list of every stone imaginable, what follows is a list of common stones and brief descriptions of each. This will help you determine the kind of stone you want to use for your projects and what's available in your area.

Alabaster: This dense translucent or white fine-grained gypsum is slightly harder than soapstone and great for carving.

Argillite: This metamorphic rock is of medium to hard density (somewhere between shale and slate) and dark red in color. It's used for building, and it's usually cut into blocky, rectangular and square shapes.

Basalt: This is a dark-colored, fine-grained igneous rock formed by the solidification of lava. There are many types of basalt distributed throughout the world. The Giants Causeway, located along the coast of Northern Ireland, is made up of an estimated 37,000 basalt columns, ranging from polygons to hexagons. Also found in the United States' Pacific Northwest, basalt is often used in water features and as water basins.

In the Pacific Northwest, U.S.A., *basalt* boulders are commonly used for building dry-laid retaining walls.

Weathered, dimensional blocks of *granite* make this covered niche an inviting spot to sit.

Feldspar: This rock-forming mineral occurs mostly in igneous rocks, and nearly 60 percent of the Earth's crust is composed of it.

Gneiss: This metamorphic rock is made up of separate layers or bandings of materials, such as quartz, feldspar, and mica. With its rustic surface quality, gneiss is a good building stone for mortared veneer and dry stone walls and can commonly be found on mountainous slopes, in fields, and in creek beds.

Granite: Often used in building and ornamental work, this heavy, coarse-grained igneous rock contains quartz and feldspar. It's one of the hardest and most durable stones.

Hornblende: This is a bluish green to black mineral found in newly formed igneous rock.

Limestone: Primarily made of calcium carbonate derived from marine sediments, this sedimentary stone is good for carving and building. Varieties of limestone include oolitic, dolomitic, and carboniferous, each distinguished from one another by texture and density.

Marble: This is a fine-to coarse-grained, crystalline rock, such as limestone, which has metamorphosed from its original form by heat and pressure.

Quartz: This is a common mineral consisting primarily of silica, a compound of silicon and oxygen. Quartz is present in many rocks and appears as speckling in granite and as bands in stones such as gneiss and hornblende.

Quartzite: This is metamorphosed sandstone that's extremely hard and nonporous. It contains up to 90 percent quartz. Though considered a hard stone, it tends to shatter when struck with a hammer. Quartzite

Stone carver Tom Jackson renders architectural features from Indiana *limestone*. The consistency of this oolitic limestone makes it a predictable material to carve.

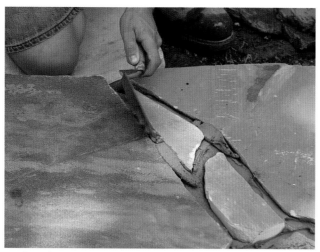

Medium-density split *sandstone* has a gritty surface, which is ideal for mortared or dry-laid paving.

THE LANGUAGE OF STONE

BEFORE VISITING YOUR LOCAL STONE YARD or stone supplier, familiarize yourself with the terms stonemasons use. It'll make discussing what you're looking for a whole lot easier, and professionals tend to appreciate amateurs who know what they're talking about before wandering into a stone yard. Also, refer to this glossary as you're reading this book.

Aggregate: This is a common term describing crushed, sharp-edged quarried stone, such as ³⁄₈-inch (1 cm) pea gravel and larger pieces up to 1¹⁄₂ inches (3.8 cm), used in concrete mixtures and road bond. Larger aggregate, such as railroad ballast, is 2¹⁄₂ inches (6.4 cm) in size and makes a good base for paths in damp, boggy soil. It's also good for filling in driveway potholes.

Anchors (or deadmen): These are long stones that are set randomly into retaining walls, with their lengths positioned across, rather than along, the length of the wall. Because their back ends extend into the gravel backfill, they anchor the wall.

makes a good border around garden beds, and larger weathered pieces make interesting viewing stones.

Sandstone: This is a porous sedimentary stone with a consistent crystalline structure. Sandstone of medium density is an excellent choice for mortared and dry-laid stonework. It's easy to break and trim with a hammer, and it's also suitable for stone carving.

Schist: This is a metamorphic rock composed of flaky, relatively parallel layers of minerals, including iron and mica.

Shale: This is a soft rock composed of layers of compacted, fine-grained, clay, silt, or mud sediments.

Slate: This metamorphic rock was fine clay that has been metamorphosed by heat and pressure. This dense, fine-grained stone readily splits into thin, smooth pieces commonly used for roofing, mortared paving, and kitchen countertops.

Soapstone: This is a soft, metamorphic rock composed mostly of talc. It has a smooth, soapy feel, and it's great for carving.

Large pieces of fieldstone make substantial *capstones* for this dry-stacked retaining wall.

An even row of neatly stacked single *coping stones*.

stones are set vertically in a series that's either plumb or at a slight angle (around 15°).

Corbel: This is a cantilevered stone supported at only one end. It's often stacked two or more on top of one another, stepping out as they rise.

Cornerstones: Stacked at wall ends and set at outside corners of coursed stonework, these stones have two faces 90° from each other.

Courses: These are the horizontal layers of stones in any mortared or dry-stacked stone wall.

Crushed stone: This is quarried stone, such as pea gravel or larger aggregates.

Ashlar: This is quarried stone that has been cut to specific dimensions and laid in deliberate patterns with consistent mortar joints.

Berm: This is a raised bank of soil. It can also be a mound of earth placed against the wall of a building to provide protection or insulation.

Bond stones: These are stones that break vertical joints and extend well into a wall in order to give structural integrity to stonework.

Boulder: A boulder is simply any rock that's too heavy for one peron to lift by hand.

Capstones: These are the uppermost stones on a wall (laid horizontally). They're used to finish a wall and protect the stonework.

Chinking stones: These are small stones or broken pieces that are used to fill in gaps in wide joints between larger stones.

Coping stones: These are the uppermost stones on a wall, most often set on top of the capstone course. Used on both freestanding and retaining walls, these

Carefully selected *cornerstones* are used here to make a stout stone post at a wall's end.

This dressed, *dimensional stone* laid in an *ashlar* pattern has a bold, rough-pitched surface that complements the size of the stone.

Dimensional stone: This is stone that's quarried and cut to an exact size and shape. Granite, marble, and limestone are common dimensional stones used in architectural stonework.

Dressed stone: This is dimensional stone that has had a particular texture, motif, or pattern worked on the stone's face.

Face: A stone's face is the surface chosen to be exposed when set into vertical stonework, such as a wall.

Fieldstones: These are stones found loose on the ground or embedded in the soil. They often appear mysteriously each spring as the frozen ground pushes them to the surface. You can use fieldstones as stepping stones, pavers, and wall stones. Weathered fieldstone is preferred in most cases, particularly for boulderscaping and stones set in Japanese-style gardens.

Flagstone: Also referred to as flagging, a flagstone is any stone used for paving, including fieldstone, random or cut sandstone, and slate.

Glacial erratics: These are stones that have wandered from their place of origin by way of glacial movement.

Gravel (washed crushed stone): This is $\frac{3}{8}$- to $1\frac{1}{2}$ inch (1 to 3.8 cm) crushed stone.

Igneous rock: This is a rock formed from reservoirs of molten lava made up of crystallized minerals. It solidifies at the earth's surface or by extreme pressure below the Earth. Granite is the preeminent igneous rock, noted for its hardness and lasting qualities.

Joint: A joint is the space between any two stones in a stone structure. There are horizontal joints between courses of stonework and vertical joints between stones in each course.

Metamorphic rock: This is stone that was originally igneous or sedimentary but has changed in appearance and character through the natural forces of heat, pres-

Most stone yards will have bulk piles of building stone, such as this selection of fieldstone.

sure, and water. Granite could become gneiss; limestone could recrystallize into marble; shale might be transformed by pressure into slate.

Pea gravel: These are small, round, and smooth stones dredged from rivers. Often small, ⅜-inch (1 cm) crushed quarry stone is also called pea gravel.

Plumb: This means that a wall is exactly vertical.

Quarried stone: This is stone that has been cut, broken, or blasted from bedrock. Large blanks, weighing up to 15 tons (13.5 t) are then split, sawed, and broken into building, paving, and dimensional cut stone.

Quoin stone: This is a dimensionally cut cornerstone used for wall ends and window and door openings.

River rocks: These are rocks that have been rounded by the relentless force of water.

The thin *shim stone* set between the two larger stones is used to level the top stone.

River slicks: These are small, mostly flat, stones with rounded edges and smooth surfaces.

Rock: A rock is any naturally formed solid material made of the earth's crust or petrified matter.

Rock dust: This is the screening from washed and sieved crushed stone, such as pea gravel (also called quarry screening).

Road bond (ABC or crusher run): This is a mixture of crushed stone, ⅜ to 1½ inches (1 to 3.8 cm) in size, and rock dust, which binds the mix together. Commonly used to build dirt roads or as a base for paved roads, road bond compacts well and is good for building up low spots in paving projects.

Rubble stones: These are irregularly shaped stones without obvious faces. Rubble stones are best used as backfill behind retaining walls and rough mortared stonework.

Smooth, rounded stones, referred to as *river slicks*, are used to dress up paving projects and water features, adding interesting colors and textures.

A *talus slope* in British Columbia, Canada.

stone, river stone, building stone, millstones, and cobblestones.

Stretchers: These stones have long, horizontal faces and are usually used to lay on top of smaller stones in the course beneath them in order to break several joints with one stone.

Talus (Scree): This is a mass of broken stones and boulders that accumulates at the base of a cliff or mountain slope.

Through or tie stones: These stones will have a length equal to or slightly longer than the width of a freestanding wall. They are laid across the width of a wall at regular intervals every 3 feet (.9 m), midway in the wall's height in order to provide extra structural integrity.

Wedges: These are small tapered bits of stone used to level larger stones, either from front to back or side to side. Whenever you trim stones, save the broken-off pieces, especially tapered ones, to serve as wedges.

There are, of course, other terms you'll become familiar with as you experience the many techniques and projects in this book.

Running joint: A running joint occurs when the joints in a series of courses fall along the same vertical line, creating a weak spot in the stonework.

Sedimentary stone: This stone is created by the settling of layer upon layer of sediments deposited at the bottom of a body of water, such as an ocean or lake. The layers, referred to as *strata*, vary from a fraction of an inch to 10 feet (3 m) in thickness, with pressure and heat forming the stone. Limestone and sandstone are both sedimentary.

Shim stones: These are small, thin, and relatively flat pieces of stone that are used to adjust the overall height of larger stones.

Stone: Rock that has been shaped by natural forces or by human persuasion, including natural weathered

The *through* or *tie stone* is the long stone extending well beyond the other wall stones. It helps to tie together the stonework and the packed crushed stone.

THE SEARCH FOR STONE

FOR MANY ARTISTS AND MASONS, finding the right material for a particular project is as satisfying as viewing the completed work. It's a great feeling when the stone you have searched for and selected complements and enhances your project. The easiest and most direct route to a stone supply is to look in the business section of your phone directory under "Stone." You can also check other nearby towns and cities for locations.

A great deal has happened in the stone supply industry over the past 20 years. Every year, the number of stone suppliers has increased, making material more widely available. For years, stone yards were used to dealing primarily with stonemasons, building contractors, landscape architects, and landscaping professionals. These days, more and more homeowners are choosing to become involved in building their homes and creating their own landscapes. In response to this trend, many yards are making their businesses more visually appealing and finding more sophisticated and attractive ways of presenting stone to the general public.

Competition in the stone market has also created one-stop shopping centers for a wide variety of building stone, ornamental stone, pea stone, pavers, stone sculpture, Asian garden features, tools, and more. I visited one stone yard in Seattle, Washington, that left my head spinning after wandering through acres of stone. With this in mind, be prepared to make at least a couple of trips to the local stone yard before making any final decisions on your building materials and tools. If you have more than one stone supplier in your area, compare prices and quality. Sometimes stone yards and landscape suppliers will have brochures describing their stone and their masonry/landscape services; many have websites.

One ton (.9 t) wire baskets of building stone in a stone yard.

Dimensional Stone

Some stone suppliers have the ability to custom cut and shape stone. Extremely large blocks of stone are first reduced to smaller cubes using feather wedges and hammers. Then, large wet saws and stone guillotines are used to create more specific shapes. This type of work is common for producing dimensional building stone, such as blocks of stone for carving and custom pavers.

Purchasing Stone

Stone is sold by weight. Often you'll find stone stacked on a pallet and enclosed in wire baskets or wrapped with plastic with a tag stating the weight. These pallets of hand-selected stone are usually sold as a unit. There have been times when I've only needed half a basket's worth to complete a job and was allowed to pick off the top half. Be sure to ask first before removing any stones from baskets.

Stone yards that deal in high volumes of stone may have a drive-on scale. In this situation, you drive your vehicle onto the scale before your stone is loaded to get your vehicle's empty weight. With the vehicle loaded, a second weight will tell how much stone you're buying. Another common method for weighing stone is a scale on which the pallets of stone are individually placed. For this, the stone yard will have a forklift to move the pallets around.

Handpicking Stone

Sometimes it's worth the effort to handpick your stone from bulk piles. I recommend handpicking particular pieces of stone, such as cornerstones and capstones for walls, treadstones for steps, specialty stones for water features, and landscaping boulders. Handpicking will take extra time, but once you know what to look for, it'll be time well spent. If you need more than a couple of tons of stone, you may want to buy some already on pallets and handpick the more specific stones. If the pile of bulk stone you want to pick through is small or looks picked over, ask when they'll be getting another load and come back then.

There's no guarantee that a stone yard or landscape supplier will have the stone you want when you want it. Plan in advance, and when you find what you're looking for, be prepared to purchase it then. The stone yard may be willing to hold the stone for a week or two if you're not ready for its delivery, providing the yard has the space.

If you're choosing landscape stones that are heavier than you can pick up, you may need to bring a friend along or ask for assistance from someone working at the yard. Most stone yards will have a forklift or front

Stone is available in a wide variety of textures and colors.

loader and an operator available. To identify and hold large landscape boulders, you'll need to mark them with surveyors' tape or a small spot of bright removable paint. (I go for the neon colors.) The paint can be removed with a wire brush.

If a stone yard has bulk piles of stone to choose from, most likely they'll charge you a nominal hand-picking fee over the price per ton. One stone yard I go to has a "select" pile of stone that has a premium price. When this particular sandstone is gathered, it's graded as the truck is filled. I will spend less time picking through this pile, though I'll spend more money on the stone. The difference in the choices between the same stone in a random pile and the select one is considerable. Often I will pick through both piles.

HANDPICKING POINTERS

Most stone yards will have you stack the stone on wooden pallets that are stacked up around the yard. If you have a small-bed pickup, you may have to hunt for a narrow pallet. The standard size pallet fits well in the bed of full-size trucks. Lay a couple of pallets out in front of the pile you're picking from. As you collect a group of stones set them on a pallet.

Stack the stones in a deliberate manner so they won't come spilling off as the pallet is set on the weigh scale. Set your largest stones along the outside edges of the pallet. Pack medium and smaller stones in the center. Create a pyramid of sorts with each course of stone tapering toward the middle. Don't overload one pallet; use two or more instead. With the forklift, someone from the stone yard will weigh the pallet and then load

Large blocks of sandstone weighing 10 to 15 tons (9 to 13.5 t) are split and sawed into pieces of flagstone.

Set your selected stones on pallets carefully so the stones don't fall over when the pallet is lifted.

it into your truck or onto one of the yard's for delivery. Delivery charges are an added expense, so try to have your order sent on one truck.

What to Bring with You

If you're going to the stone yard to select and purchase stone, there are a few things to wear and take along. Wear sturdy shoes or work boots, work clothes, and take a pair of leather gloves. To test how a particular stone breaks or splits, bring a 3-pound (1.4 kg) hammer, which is fine to do, just don't get carried away with it. Also bring along a measuring tape.

I've seen stone hauled out of the stone yard in the trunk of a car, though don't expect to haul much stone this way. A small half-ton truck will haul more stone and is much easier to load and unload.

Other Sources of Stone

If you live in a rocky area, there may be private and public lands you can visit in order to pick stone or

boulders for free or a small fee. I don't advise picking stone off of someone's property without getting the owner's permission first.

If you've found some stone, and it's not obvious who the owner is, do a little investigating. Ask people on the neighboring property, or if you can locate the property on a map, the local deed office can find the owner from tax records. If you live in a fairly rural setting, stone should be easy to find simply by asking around. There may be an active quarry in the area or old stone farm walls someone is eager to get rid of.

QUARRY SITES

Abandoned quarry sites are excellent locations to find building stone, carving stones (limestone quarries), landscape boulders, and standing stones. If the quarry is completely abandoned, you'll have to locate the current owner and ask if they're willing to open the quarry for you.

SCREE AND TALUS

Scree and talus are terms that describe rocks of all sizes that accumulate at the base of a rocky slope. Usually there's a bold rock face at the top of the slope with an area clear of trees and vegetation below where the stones gather. The physical geography of this type of setting is easy to locate by sight, and if it's easy to get a truck there, you may be able to gather an excellent selection of stone. Extreme caution should be used when walking across these slopes. The stones are loose and still subject to movement. The safest place to pick is toward the bottom of the slope.

HOUSE SITES

Old house sites can also provide good stone, but be cautious of stone that has been through a fire. The intense heat may have weakened the stone. You may

Although partially obscured by mosses and ferns, the walls of this abandoned quarry offer a glimpse of the local geology.

Most stone is chosen with consideration for its color, texture, strength, and price. A stone's workability is also something to consider, particularly if you're new to stonework. When selecting stone for a particular project, you need to consider the availability of a good selection of shapes and sizes. Even with a good selection of stone, it's likely you'll have to shape some of the stones by breaking and trimming to fit them properly into a wall or paving project.

Once you've worked with stone, it will forever change the way you look at it. Physically handling a stone gives you an immediate appreciation of its weight and density. Each stone is unique, which is what makes working with stone both challenging and interesting. Breaking a stone in two across its grain or splitting it into thinner layers along its grain reveals more information about the stone's structure. When you have moved, sorted, split, broken, shaped, moved again, and finally stacked a ton of stone, you'll begin to know that particular type of stone, appreciate its qualities, and anticipate its limitations.

come across an old mortared stone foundation that will require a pry bar or a digging bar to loosen the stones. A scaling hammer is used specifically to remove old mortar from brick and stone. A brick mason's hammer will also work.

The Perfect Stone

There is such a thing as the perfect building stone. I describe it as one that I don't have to move more than once or twice before it's set in a wall. When searching for stone for a project, you'll most likely want to use the stone already available at the local stone yard, unless you have an unlimited budget. Avoid stones that are soft and crumble at their edges; they won't weather well or hold up under the weight of other stones.

Chapter 2

TOOLS &
BASIC TECHNIQUES

*f*or me, there is something primal about breaking stone that often evokes memories of ancient ancestry. Sometimes my thoughts turn to my great-great-grandfather, Truxton Reed, a stonecutter who worked in the New England states and was involved in building the Erie Canal. In my mind, I often wander back to his era and imagine myself working with stone at that time, realizing that the basic tool design hasn't changed much since then. Stones mark the beginning of primitive tool technology. Strike two stones together and eventually one stone will break against the other, leaving fragments with sharp edges. These sharp-edged flakes were used to collect and process food and work other materials such as wood or animal hides. The earliest hammers were simply stones weighing 2 to 3 pounds (.9 to 1.4 kg) gripped against the palm of the hand. The point here is not to impart knowledge of primitive tools, but to remember the simple beauty of this ancient material we're using. When you think about it, a steel hammerhead with a wooden handle is still a simple tool.

GETTING STARTED

MOST OF THE TOOLS YOU'LL NEED for the projects in this book are simple, fairly inexpensive, and easy to maintain. Hardware stores and home improvement centers carry everything you need, and I've found many of my tools at flea markets, antique stores, and yard sales. The stone-working techniques detailed here are also simple and designed to get the job done safely and effectively.

TO GET STARTED WITH A DRY-LAID
PROJECT, YOU'LL NEED THESE BASIC TOOLS:
Stonemason's hammer, 2 to 3 pounds (.9 to 1.4 kg)
Brick-and-block mason's hammer, 1 to 2 pounds
(.45 to .9 kg)
Cold chisel, 8 inches (20.3 cm) long
Wheelbarrow
Shovel
Mattock
Tamper
Several 5-gallon (19 L) buckets
Heavy-duty work gloves
Safety glasses

FOR A MORTARED PROJECT,
YOU'LL ALSO NEED:
Mortar hoe
Mason's trowels*
Brick trowel, 4½ x 9 inches (11.4 x 22.9 cm)
Gauging trowel, 3⅜ x 7 inches (8.6 x 17.8 cm)
Pointing trowels
Hose with a nozzle
Gas or electric mortar mixer, for larger projects
* I prefer smaller trowels. They're easier to work
with when setting mortar behind the stonework.

More specific tools will be listed, as they're needed for each project, and tools and techniques for lifting boulders appear on page 149.

LIFTING, HAULING, AND CARRYING STONE

WHETHER YOU'RE WORKING WITH GRAVEL or boulders, you need a safe and effective way to get your stones to your work site.

Wheelbarrows

A stout, metal wheelbarrow is a must for moving stones. The standard barrow (or pan) sizes are 4 and 6 cubic feet (.12 and .18 m³). I prefer the larger model, which can also be used for mixing mortar. The plastic barrows will work; however, they don't hold up to a lot of abuse. Two-wheeled wooden garden carts are capable of handling light loads, though the wheel rims and axles on these carts can't withstand heavy loads. A wooden brick barrow has the identical frame and single wheel of a wheelbarrow, but its barrow is made of wooden slats and designed more like a cart. The wooden slats cover the bottom, with three of the sides left open, making it easier to load and unload bags of mortar and loads of stone. No matter what type of barrow you choose, it should have a large pneumatic tire, which will give you more control over uneven ground.

The brickbarrow is a sturdy and lightweight cousin of the standard wheelbarrow and is ideal for moving stones and bags of cement.

USING A WHEELBARROW

To move very large stones, first turn the wheelbarrow on edge, right next to the stone. Push the stone into the barrow. Then lift the stone up onto its end and move around to the other side of the wheelbarrow. Pull the wheelbarrow and stone toward you until the wheelbarrow is upright.

For moving heavy loads up an incline, have a second person in front grabbing the lip of the barrow while pulling upward and forward at the same time. If there's only one person, zigzag up a slope when possible or take lighter loads. Having the correct tire pressure is crucial for these maneuvers.

Centering heavy materials directly over a wheelbarrow's tire lightens the load on the handles.

Hand Trucks and Ball Carts

A small hand truck with pneumatic tires is easy to handle and capable of hauling 200 to 300 pounds (91 to 136 kg). If your work site if fairly level, you can load large, blocky stones, capstones, or small boulders on a hand truck and move them wherever they're needed. Ball carts have a larger metal frame and bigger tires than the hand truck. They're designed to move trees and shrubs with bulky root balls. I've found them to be extremely helpful when moving large slabs of stone weighing 200 to 300 pounds (91 to 136 kg) each. Your local nursery or tree farm may have a ball cart they'd be willing to lend or rent, or they could direct you to a source for purchasing one.

Moving larger pieces of stone often requires larger equipment. While still manually operated, a ball cart is capable of moving these 250-pound (113.5 kg) slabs of flagstone.

USING A HAND TRUCK OR BALL CART

To use either the hand truck or ball cart, position it as close as possible to the stone you're going to move. With its frame or lip along the bottom front edge at ground level, slide the edge underneath the stone. Center the stone on the cart and tilt the truck back slightly toward you. Then either push or pull it in the direction you want to go.

A stack of building stone can be moved about easily with a small handtruck.

Buckets

Five-gallon (19 L) buckets can often be found on construction sites, at bakeries, and for sale at home improvement centers. They're invaluable for hauling gravel, sand, water, and for collecting smaller stones. I store my hammers and chisels in them, and I turn empty buckets upside down when I need a seat.

Ramps

Pieces of lumber, 4 to 8 feet (1.2 to 2.4 m) long, make good ramps when you need to move large stones into a truck bed or when setting large capstones on a retaining wall.

A four-foot-long (1.2 m) ramp using a 4 x 4 piece of lumber

USING A RAMP

For moving large building stones or capstones from ground level up onto a wall, set one end of the ramp on the wall. Slide the stone onto the board and stand it up on its edge. Then, walk it up the ramp or flip it end over end up the ramp. Two people working together can slide a stone up the inclined board.

Log Rollers

Also keep a few 3-foot-long (.9 m) round logs, 4 to 10 inches (10.2 to 25.4 cm) in diameter, on hand, to serve as wheels for rolling large flat stones from one place to another.

USING LOG ROLLERS

You'll need four log ends that are perfectly round for moving large slabs. If the stone has at least one flat side, it can be moved with just log rollers. For irregular-shaped stones, build a simple stone boat made with 4 x 4-inch (10.2 x 10.2 cm) timbers as runners connected with a 2 x 5-foot (.6 x 1.5 m) plywood deck.

Moving a stone using long rollers is much easier and more fun with at least two people. Set the stone boat on the ground alongside the stone you're moving, pointed in the direction you want to move the stone. To set the stone on the boat, use two digging bars and blocks of wood as levers and fulcrums. As you lift the stone, chuck blocks of wood underneath. Lift the stone up to the height of the boat, then slide it onto the plywood deck.

You can also use lumber as "tracks" for your rollers.

Using the levers and fulcrum, pry up on the front of the runners high enough to slip a log roller underneath. Push from the opposite end using the pry bar, if needed, rolling it a couple of feet, then setting another log roller at the front of the boat. Keep positioning the rollers at the front and pushing the boat along, gathering rollers from the rear to be set in the front as needed.

Lifting Stones by Yourself

Building stones are moved a minimum of three times: when they're gathered and delivered, when they're sorted out at the project site, and finally, when they're set in the project. The effect on the body of picking up one stone after another is cumulative and really only something to worry about if you're choosing this as a career. Start a project slowly, stretch out before and after working, and consider the following tips:

• The proper way to lift a stone is by crouching down with your knees bent and back straight. Pick up the stone and stand up, using your leg muscles to lift while holding the stone close to your body. Use this method with particularly heavy stones, and avoid twisting the upper body while you're lifting. Bending over to pick up smaller stones is fine, just be mindful of what you're doing.

• When crouched down about to lift a heavy stone, first take a couple of deep breaths and focus your attention on your body lifting the stone.

• For walking with a heavy stone, hold it close to you, resting it on an upper thigh if you need to.

• When two or more people are lifting a large stone, first agree on which direction you're going and take slow steady steps together.

POUNDING AND BREAKING STONE

NO MATTER HOW MANY TIMES YOU READ about breaking stone, you won't know how to break stone until you do it, and do it, and do it. After a lot of practice, you'll learn just where to grip the handle of your hammer in relationship to the power your arm is delivering with its swing. As your hand-to-eye coordination improves, you'll notice the stones breaking where you want them to more often. Using a banker or a pile of sand or gravel on the ground is helpful when you're first starting out (see page 34).

Hammers

There are a number of hammers in the 1- to 4-pound (.45 to 1.8 kg) range that stonemasons use to break and split stone, including brick-and-block mason's hammers, stonemason's hammers, mash hammers, and blacksmith's forging hammers. Of the dozen or so hammers that I currently own, my favorites are a 2½-pound (1.1 kg) **blacksmith's forging hammer** and a 3-

Stonemason's hammers

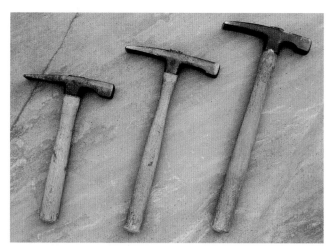

Brick-and-block mason's hammers

pound (1.4 kg) **stonemason's hammer** (also referred to as a **spalling hammer**). You can use both of these hammers to break away large sections of unwanted stone.

The **mash hammer** comes in 2-, 3-, and 4-pound (.9, 1.4, and 1.8 kg) weights and is my hammer of choice when using chisels to split a stone with the grain or to score a stone for breaking across the grain. A 4-pound (1.8 kg) **bush hammer**, with a deep-grooved waffle head, is handy for evening out the high spots on the surfaces of softer stones, such as sandstone. A 3-pound (1.4 kg) **rubber or leather mallet** is useful for setting mortared flagstone and other paving materials. The lighter hammers such as the **brick-and-block mason's hammers** work well for trimming smaller stones and thinner sections of stone. **Sledgehammers** are the heavy hitters, weighing 4 to 16 pounds (1.8 to 7.3 kg). They're generally used to make smaller stones out of big ones. My 5- and 12-pound (2.3 and 5.4 kg) sledges see the most use; occasionally I'll use my 16-pound (7.3 kg) hammer to break extremely thick or dense stones, such as granite.

The waffle-head of a bush hammer can also be used to leave a highly textured surface on carved limestone.

Sledgehammers weighing 16, 12, and 5 pounds (7.3, 5.4, and 2.3 kg), respectively

SHAPING AND SPLITTING STONE

Successfully shaping and/or splitting a stone without shattering it is that mysterious part of stonework that most people find so fascinating. Stone responds to the striking of a hammer according to its density and structural makeup. I do most of my stone shaping by gripping the stone with my right hand and bracing it against my right thigh (I'm left-handed). Set up stones that are too heavy to hold on a banker (see page 34). Remember to always wear safety glasses when using hammers and chisels.

A 2.5-pound blacksmith's hammer was used to break away the tapered edge of a piece of flagging.

To trim a tapered edge or remove a section of stone, turn the stone's edge you're working on slightly out and away from you. Strike the outside edge of the stone with the squared end of the hammerhead. Thin the stone's thickness first from this angle, then flip it over and continue thinning the stone so it has a tapered edge. Strike the thinned edge back to square up its edge, showing the thickness of the stone again. Repeat if more of the stone needs to be removed.

Some stones will have one or more natural fissures or clefts along their bedding seams. To split a small stone along its seam with a hammer, stand the stone up on edge so the seam is facing up. Then, using the

Striking this stone several times along a visible seam caused the stone to crack and then neatly separate into two pieces.

tapered end of a stonemason's hammer, strike along the seam until it opens up and the stone splits. To split a stone with a large surface area, such as a capstone or flagstone, read the section on using chisels (page 30).

The deep-grooved waffle head of a bush hammer acts like a grid of small-pointed chisels. When the waffle head strikes a high spot on a stone's surface, it breaks the surface up into smaller pieces. Repeated striking pulverizes the high spot, creating an even surface. This is a good way to round off the sharp edge on a stone, as well.

MAKING SMALLER STONES

A general rule of thumb is that the larger the stone you want to break, the bigger the hammer you'll need. This is particularly true in relation to a stone's thickness. The weight of a sledgehammer's head and its long handle create a dynamic force when struck against stone. Sometimes you get the stone to break just the way you want it to, though often you'll end up with a bunch of smaller pieces that make good backfill in a retaining wall or core material for a freestanding wall.

For the best control of the hammer, crouch down in front of the stone, raise the hammer above your head, and strike the stone where you want it to

A 12-pound (5.4 kg) sledgehammer splitting a piece of dense sandstone

break. For an even rift (break) of stones with a large surface area, strike at several points along the line you want to crack. A 5- to 10-pound (2.3 to 4.5 kg) sledgehammer will work for most situations. I once had to break large 6-inch-thick (15.2 cm) slabs of granite into squared corners for a couple of mortared-stone gateposts. A 20-pound (9 kg) sledge was required in that situation.

Stonemason Jeff Thue using a sledgehammer to split a boulder

CUTTING, SCORING, SPLITTING, AND CHIPPING STONE

CHISELS ARE USED FOR SCORING, SPLITTING, CUTTING, and chipping stone. Although a hammer will work alone to split or break stone, in some situations, using the correct chisel gives you more control.

Chisels

The least expensive chisels for stonework are **cold chisels**, 8 to 10 inches (20 to 25 cm) long, with shafts about ¾ inch (2 cm) in diameter and blades ranging

From left to right: a brick chisel and three cold chisels

from 1 to 2 inches wide (2.5 to 5.1 cm). (Note the end of the blade of a cold chisel will be beveled on both sides of the cutting edge.) Also in this category is a **brick chisel**, with a wider blade of 3 inches (7.6 cm).

The chisels used by professional stonemasons are heavier, will last longer, and are three to four times more expensive than the standard cold chisels. Made of alloy steel, these professional tools are also available

From left to right: a hand-point chisel, a hand-set chisel, and a hand-tracer chisel

with carbide tips that hold an edge 20 times longer than regular steel.

The three basic chisels used by professional stonemasons are the **hand point**, the **hand tracer**, and the **hand sets**. These chisels are available through masonry supply businesses and some home hardware stores.

USING CHISELS

Hand point chisels are used to chisel away high spots on a stone. They're also useful for tracing lines and chipping off edges on a stone. A hand set has a blunt, squared edge that's good for breaking away unwanted sections of stone. Hand tracers are used to score straight lines on stones and split stone. Many types of stone (sedimentary, in particular) have visible bedding seams that can be split, making thinner pieces of stone.

To split a stone with a hammer and hand tracer, stand the stone up on edge, and set it either on the ground or on a banker (see page 34). Place the chisel's cutting edge along the seam you want to split. Tap the chisel with a 2- to 3-pound (.9 to 1.4 kg) hammer, moving the chisel along the seam from one end to the next, repeating the chiseling along the seam until it

starts to open. Turn the stone until the opposite end is up, and chisel along the same seam. As it starts to open, the ringing of the stone and chisel will turn to a dull thud. At that point, the stone should split into two pieces. For large stones, start the cleft with the chisel, working it along the length of the seam, until you get an opening. Then use a few jimmy wedges set out along the seam, with the tapered ends placed in the cleft. Tap each wedge evenly into the seam until the stone splits.

Jimmy wedges

The hand point chisel directs the force from a hammer into its single point. To lift high spots from a stone's surface, chisel with the point around the section you're removing. Chisel into the center of a high spot, changing the angle of the chisel as it breaks up. Continue chiseling from the edges and into the center, and then use a cold chisel or tracer to even the surface out.

Hand sets, with their blunt, squared cutting edges, are useful for breaking away large sections along the edge of a stone. I use one exclusively for shaping 2-inch-thick (5.1 cm) sandstone pavers. While kneeling on the paver, move the chisel along the outside edge, chipping away small sections of stone with each strike from a hammer. Angle the striking end of the chisel toward you, putting the cutting edge in the opposite direction, which is where you want the stone chips to fly.

Saws

A double-insulated electrical circular saw rated at 13 amps or more, with a 7¼-inch-diameter (18.4 cm) abrasive or diamond blade, is useful for scoring flagstone before you break it. Both abrasive and diamond blades work well on medium and soft stone.

A masonry cut-off saw, with an abrasive or diamond blade 12 to 14 inches (30 or 36 cm) in diameter will cut stone, concrete, or metal. These saws are similar to chainsaws, but they make use of a large disklike blade instead of a chain. They weigh around 40 pounds (18.2 kg), so they're not for everyone! Check them out at your local equipment rental center.

Not for the timid, a masonry cut-off saw is36 an aggressive tool capable of cutting through medium-density stone, concrete, or metal.

USING SAWS

Cutting stone to mark a line to be rifted (broken) or even cutting all the way through works only on medium and soft stones, such as sandstone and lime-stone.

The stone I cut most often with a saw is a medium-density sandstone used in mortared and dry-laid paving. First define the portion to be removed by using a straightedge and chisel to score a line across the stone's surface. Prop the stone up at a 15° angle, with the marked end at the lower end. Position a hose with a nozzle at the top of the stone so that you can direct a slow, steady stream of water down the stone and across the scored line. Put on your safety glasses and earplugs.

Next, using a double-insulated circular saw with an abrasive or diamond blade, cut a straight, shallow groove, ¼ inch (6 mm) deep, along the scored line. Position the front edge of the saw's baseplate on top of the stone, with the saw's guide mark over the scored line. Hold the saw at an angle so the blade doesn't touch the stone. Turn the saw on, carefully lower the spinning blade down until it touches the start of the scored line, and guide the saw gently back and forth. Don't exert any downward pressure on the blade; instead, allow the weight of the saw to do the cutting. Lifting the blade guard makes it easier to control the action of the blade. Do this with extreme care! The water flowing over the stone will reduce dust in the air as well as wear on the blade.

A steady stream of water directed at the saw's blade reduces wear and rock dust. Have a second person direct the nozzle while you saw.

Two important warnings: Make absolutely sure that your circular saw is double-insulated before you run water anywhere near it. Also, if you're plugged into an extension cord, waterproof the joint where the cord and the saw plug join by wrapping it tightly with duct tape.

The setup for using a masonry cut-off saw is similar to using a circular saw. This saw has more power, more weight, and a larger blade. It helps to have a second person holding the nozzle and directing a stream of water directly on the blade. When you're cutting, allow the spinning blade to lightly touch down on the stone.

PUTTING IT ALL TOGETHER

WHEN LAYING TIGHT STONEWORK, be it mortared or dry-laid, developing a critical eye is as important as having a good selection of stone to choose from. Once a stone is set in a wall, you don't want to have to take it back out. If there are any large protrusions that will keep the next course from being laid properly, it's best to remove them before you move on to the next stone. If you're frustrated by the choices of stone and find you're unhappy with what's laid, you may need to take some of the work out. Sloppy work looks bad by itself—when mixed with good work it looks really bad.

If you can't find a stone to fit in a particular spot, you'll have to make one fit. Start with something at least close to the shape you want. In stone wall building, the majority of the work I do to shape a stone is done with a hammer alone. Using a hammer to break and trim stone takes a certain amount of concentration and coordination. It's not difficult, but there's more to it than just swinging a hammer at a stone. Focus on where you want the hammer to hit, the angle of the hammer's head while it's swinging, and the amount of force in each swing. Fewer, more decisive strikes from hammer to stone are better than several taps. Each time you strike against a stone it sends vibrations through its structure, causing the stone to weaken. For example, if the stone is sedimentary, constant tapping may cause it to split between layers into thinner pieces.

With practice, the hammers and chisels will begin to feel more comfortable in your hands. If you need more control while working with a hammer, simply choke up on the handle. Choking up means gripping the hammer's handle closer to the hammer's head. By gripping toward the end of the hammer's handle, you'll increase the force behind each swing, but have less control.

Fresh Cuts

Any time you break a stone in two or remove a small section, it'll leave the markings of a fresh cut. Fresh cuts are most visible on weathered fieldstone and less obvious on quarried stone. Fresh cuts will take years to blend in, so keep them to a minimum, or choose to spread them out evenly throughout the stonework. Some cuts are left with sharp edges. By rounding these edges off a bit, the cut will be less obvious. Strike these sharp edges with a hammer's squared face to round them over.

OTHER TOOLS

TWO TYPES OF **SHOVELS** COME IN HANDY for grading sites and shoveling sand and gravel: one has a square blade, the other a round blade. A shovel with a square blade is most efficient for leveling rough spots of soil and shoveling sand and gravel. A shovel with a round blade works for general digging. I use shovels with short handles when I'm digging in tight spots and at odd angles.

Squared and round-point shovels

STONE BANKERS

A STONE BANKER IS ANYTHING THAT HELPS absorb the shock of a hammer blow when you're working on a stone. A stone banker will improve your ability to trim and break stones more accurately and consistently. You can create a simple banker by dumping two 5-gallon (19 L) buckets of sand or pea gravel on the ground close to where you're working. Spread the sand or gravel out evenly. The sand works best, giving an even surface for the stone to rest on while helping the stone absorb the shock from the hammer or chisel.

If you find it uncomfortable bending down while cutting or splitting stone, build this alternative:

MATERIALS
³⁄₈-inch (1 cm) plywood,
19¹⁄₂ x 19¹⁄₂ inches (49.5 x 49.5 cm)
4 pieces of 2 x 2-inch (5.1 x 5.1 cm) lumber,
19¹⁄₂ inches (49.5 cm) long
4 pieces of 2 x 2-inch (5.1 x 5.1 cm) lumber,
16¹⁄₄ inches (41.2 cm) long
Nails or screws
8 standard concrete blocks,
8 x 16 inches (20.3 x 40.6 cm)

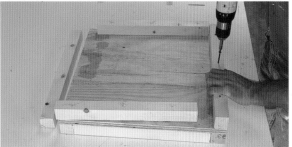

PROCEDURE

Create a rectangle in the center of the plywood with two pieces each of the 19¹⁄₂-inch (49.5 cm) and 16¹⁄₄-inch (41.2 cm) lumber. Nail or screw them into place. Flip the plywood over and repeat with the rest of the 2 x 2 pieces. Stack the concrete blocks two at a time, alternating each course to help lock them together. This will put the working surface of the banker at 32 inches (81.3 cm), a much more comfortable height in which to work. Place the banker on top of the blocks so that the 2 x 2s hold it in place underneath. Fill the banker with sand and you're ready to break some stone or carve a small piece of sculpture.

The **mattock** is similar to a miner's pickaxe, but instead of having two opposing picks, it may have either a pick or wedge-shaped blade at one end of the metal head and a slightly curved digging blade at the opposite end. This tool is useful for loosening packed earth and embedded rocks from the ground.

A **pry bar**, also referred to as a shale bar or digging bar, is a solid piece of steel, 1 to 1½ inches (2.5 to 3.8 cm) thick that's tapered at one end and beveled or wedge-shaped at the other end. It's most useful for adjusting the positions of large stones and for prying stones out of the ground. Any pry bar that doesn't bend easily is a good one. These bars vary in length from 4 to 6 feet (1.2 to 1.8 m) and weigh around 30 pounds (13.6 kg). You can locate one at your local hardware store or home improvement center.

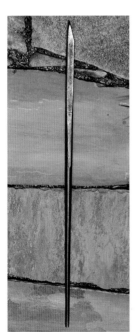

Crowbars, which are similar to pry bars, but smaller and lighter, make effective stone-prying tools. They range from 2 to 3 feet (.6 to .9 m) in length. One end of the tool is flat and slightly flared; the other end is curved in a "J" shape.

You'll need a **tamper** to compact soil or gravel for dry-laid projects. This tool is simply a flat piece of metal attached to a long handle.

A **measuring tape** is necessary to have on site. For general use, I prefer a 16- or 25-foot (4.8 or 7.5 m) tape. Longer ones are bulkier and heavier.

The wider, heavy-gauge tapes will last much longer than the narrow, flimsy ones.

You'll need at least one level for setting steps, pavers, and benches. The highest quality **levels** are made of wood and metal; less expensive ones are made of plastic. A 2-foot (61-cm) level is handy for setting step treads and adjusting individual stones within a paving project. For gauging the level and pitch of several stones in a paving project, a 4- or 6-foot (1.2 or 1.8 m) level works best.

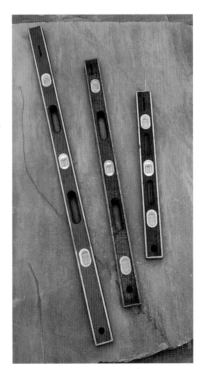

With consistent use, the edges of hammers round off, the cutting edges of chisels will blunt, and digging implements will dull. So, regular sharpening is a must. I use an electric bench grinder and a $1/3$-horsepower motor and a 6-inch (15.2 cm) grinding wheel. You can also use a belt sander and/or manually sharpen your tools with a vise and metal file. If you don't want to buy a grinder, take your tools to a professional sharpening service. Be aware that the cutting edge of a chisel does not need to be sharp like a knife's blade.

SAFETY EQUIPMENT

THERE'S NO WAY TO PREDICT which way rock chips will fly when breaking and trimming stone. For this reason, safety glasses are a must when working with stone. I discovered a lightweight pair of safety glasses that offer full protection by wrapping around the sides of my head, while still providing good ventilation. When I'm working, I keep these glasses dangling from a strap around my neck, ready to be worn at any time.

Wearing tough leather gloves while working with stone is the best way to protect your hands. Make sure they fit well; loose gloves won't let you get a good grip on stones or tools. For good support and protection, wear leather boots. When you're working on paving projects, knee pads or garden pads will save wear and tear on your trousers and knees.

Most stonework involves a lot of bending down and lifting. This requires a fair amount of stamina. I suggest starting off with a simple, small-scale project and working into it, slowly. I've avoided serious injury over the past 15 years as a stonemason, but there certainly have been a number of scrapes, bruises, and pinched fingers along the way, most of which happened when I wasn't paying attention.

BEFORE YOU BEGIN

MANY OF THE PROJECTS IN THIS BOOK are for those with beginning and intermediate levels of stoneworking skills, and a few of the projects will be a bit more challenging. With any given stone project, the building situation is going to be different because of details specific to a site, the materials used, and the level of knowledge and experience of the builder.

Sometimes a large landscape project can be broken down into smaller ones, allowing months, even years, to complete the total picture. If you are a do-it-yourselfer, then you may already have experience with this and know how realistic your goals are. Having an overall picture of what you want in your landscape is the first step, while leaving room for change to new ideas. Taking on projects yourself can be exciting, and any of these projects can be a personally rewarding experience that you can share with your family and friends.

It's a grand feeling to conceptualize a stone feature in the landscape, gather the materials, build it, and complete the project, all because you think you can. That's why I generally encourage people to start out with a small project that's doable; positive results are wonderful. Sometimes you may feel some techniques are, quite simply, over your head. Don't let that discourage you. Call on the opinion and/or services of a professional, or seek out information in books. Other times, you may feel just comfortable enough moving forward with the technique and seeing what develops. Go with your instincts, but also don't hesitate to stop and seek assistance when needed.

Chapter 3

DRY-LAID STONEWORK

If you're a purist about stonework and wouldn't even think about using mortar in between stones, then this is an excellent chapter for you. I know about the purist attitude; I've got a bit of it in me. In this section, you'll learn about methods of building that have been used and improved upon since ancient times. For wall building, these methods include selecting good stone, fitting stones tightly, and relying on the forces of gravity and friction to keep your project together.

It's interesting how you can improvise and be more creative with fewer and simpler tools. To me this is one of the wonderful things about stonework. There's nothing to plug in—just simple, no-nonsense tools that don't require pages of instructions to understand. And with stone masonry, there's more to building a wall than just setting one stone on top of another. It's a puzzle of sorts, and achieving a well-built wall to complement the landscape is the goal. Figuring how each stone fits in the puzzle and achieving a balanced design is a challenge that makes stonework so rewarding.

FREESTANDING WALLS

A dry-laid freestanding farm wall in Saunders Town, Rhode Island

PART OF THE BEAUTY OF DRY-STONE WALLS and other dry-laid projects is that you don't need elaborate footings of concrete and steel as you do with most mortared stone walls. The type of building I'll detail in this chapter allows minor amounts of settling without undermining the project's integrity. Shifting of any sort in a mortared project will cause the mortar between the stones to crack and eventually break away. When this happens, moisture seeps into the stonework, causing further damage.

There are basically two different types of dry-stone walls. One is a freestanding wall and the other is a retaining-style wall. A freestanding wall can be built almost anywhere on top of stable soil. Freestanding walls are double-sided, having two faces that are tied together using bond and through stones. Retaining walls, on the other hand, have a single face and are built with a slight lean into a bank of soil. You'll find this style of wall building in mountainous and hilly areas, or anywhere there's a bank of soil that needs to be contained.

The craft of building dry-stacked freestanding walls has been practiced around the world, and nowhere is this more evident than in the British Isles and Ireland. The agricultural communities of these areas are synonymous with stone wall building, with many walls dating back to the eighteenth century and others to prehistory. Here, a proud heritage of wall building is evident in the webwork of thousands of miles of dry stonewalls that in many regions define the landscape.

Immigrants from Ireland and the British Isles brought their wall building skills to America. In the Colonies of New England, stone was so plentiful it was considered a nuisance, and clearing stones from the land was a constant chore. It made sense to neatly stack the stones into walls that took up less space. They also proved useful as boundary markers and fences for livestock.

Reemergence of a Craft

As with most time-honored crafts, interest in building and repairing stone walls lapsed as cheaper and more expedient means of fencing in farmland became available. In fact, when I started out as a stonemason's

A freestanding single-stone fence in Southern India

apprentice in 1986, most people I came into contact with called stonework a dying art. I don't, however, hear people saying that today. And I think it's safe to say that interest in dry-stone walls and stonework of all kinds has been restored, as have many old dry-stone walls. Part of this resurgence is due to associations, such as the Dry Stone Conservancy in Lexington, Kentucky, The Dry Stone Walling Association of Great Britain, and The Stone Foundation in Santa Fe, New Mexico. These associations offer workshops and apprenticeships that are cultivating new interest in keeping traditional wall-building skills alive and the level of craftsmanship to the highest standard possible.

Freestanding walls are referred to by different names around the world. In parts of the British Isles, Ireland, and the New England states they're called stone walls or field walls, while in Kentucky they're called rock fences. In Scotland they're called dykes. Those who build stone walls go by the titles of masons, wallers, and dykers, with the specific building terminology and wall vernacular varying from one region to the next. The basic building techniques, however, are universal.

Capped off with a cover course of stout stones, this wall's serpentine shape blends effortlessly into its woodland surroundings.

Building a Freestanding Wall

The wall detailed here is 4 feet (1.2 m) high, 2 feet (.6 m) thick at its base and 24 feet (7.2 m) long. Of course yours can be any size you desire.

CONSIDERATIONS

Freestanding walls can be anywhere from 3 to 6 feet (.9 to 1.8 m) tall. They make great privacy walls and garden borders and look wonderful in a landscape. With their double facing and stout stone footings, freestanding walls are a bit more involved than retaining walls (see page 54) of the same height and will take more time to build. So, when starting out, don't overcommit yourself to a project you don't have the time to complete. Try a short length of double-stone walling before tackling a larger project.

A dry-laid freestanding wall relies on its batter, gravity, a tight fitting of stones, a thoroughly packed center (core), and through and bond stones to bind the two faces of the wall together. Water that manages to enter the wall (properly set capstones prevent most water from entering in the first place) exits easily. A well-built wall will last at least a couple hundred years, needing only minimum maintenance.

SELECTING STONE

When selecting stone for your wall, choose relatively flat stones that are 4 to 24 inches (10.2 to 61 cm) wide and 2 to 6 inches (5.1 to 15.2 cm) thick. There are also some specific sizes and shapes of stone you'll need to be aware of when you go to gather your wall-building material:

• Your foundation stones will be the largest and heaviest stones. They should be fairly flat and similar in thickness.

• Bond stones, reaching across about two-thirds of the wall's thickness, further bind the two faces of a wall in the wall's interior. These stones will be set as often as possible with at least one every 4 feet (1.2 m) from one side to the next as the courses of stone are being stacked.

Volunteers from the Dry Stone Conservancy in Lexington, Kentucky, admiring their handiwork

• Your through stones need to span the complete width of the wall. These stones are placed every few feet along the course that is midway in the wall's height. Through stones that extend several inches beyond the wall's face on each side of the wall provide maximum strength.

• Capstones, also referred to as the "cover course," are laid horizontally along the top of a wall, binding the upper course of face stones together. One way to finish the wall is by laying single capstones that span the width of the wall. These stones will be around 16 inches (40.6 cm) wide, allowing for a 1-inch (2.5 cm) overhang on both sides, while butting up to each other as they're set.

• Traditionally, this type of wall is completed with a row of coping stones set on top of the capstones. Relatively thin coping stones are stood up vertically like books on a shelf or at an angle of 15°. The two different styles of coping are single and double copes. For single cope stones, the ideal height is 10 to 12 inches (25.4 to 30.5 cm). Single copes should span the entire surface of the last leveled face course or the top of the capstones. Double cope stones are slightly smaller, standing 8 to 10 inches (20.3 to 25.4 cm) tall.

HOW MUCH STONE YOU'LL NEED

With 1 ton (.9 t) of stone, you can build a section of wall 3 feet (.9 m) long, 2 feet (.6 m) wide at the base, and 4 feet (1.2 m) tall. For a wall 12 feet (3.6 m) long, you'll need 4 tons (3.6 t) of stones that have relatively flat top and bottom surfaces, 4 to 24 inches (10.2 to 61 cm) wide and 2 to 6 inches (5.1 to 15.2 cm) thick.

SHAPING STONES FOR WALLS

This information is useful for any type of wall you build, dry-laid or mortared (even veneered). Refer to Chapter 2 for details on how to use your tools to trim stone.

The main thing to remember when trimming stones for a wall is that a stone's fit isn't complete until each stone around it is also set. Ideally, the base and sides of each stone should be perpendicular to the stone's face. If the sides aren't squared up, you'll need to trim the stone as needed to fit with the surrounding stones. The top and bottom surfaces of a stone you're setting in a wall should be free of any protrusions that decrease its contact with surrounding stones and would cause it to wobble. An even surface will have better contact with the previous course and the following one. Most stones will need to be worked with a hammer and or shimmed with smaller stones to achieve a proper fit. It may take a minor tap with a hammer to square the thin edge of a stone, or you might have to dramatically alter the stone's shape by breaking away a large section (figure 1).

Figure 1

As you work, remember that the top portion of the stones you're setting will have to be dealt with when you're laying the next course. The heights of two adjacent stones need to match up where they meet, forming a vertical joint. If they don't, smaller stones can be used to make up the difference, or one of the stones may need to be trimmed (figure 2). Marking the portion of stone to be trimmed with a crayon is helpful when first learning to shape the stones with a hammer.

Figure 2: Two small stones can be used when a shorter stone is set between two larger ones.

Any stone trimming should be done off the wall, with the stone placed on a banker (see page 34).

When I'm wall building, I'll look for a stone that closely matches the shape of the next space to fill. I'll place the stone I've chosen on the wall with the most obvious face showing. If the fit doesn't feel right, I might flip the stone over or spin it around and show another face.

HEIGHT AND WIDTH PROPORTIONS

The freestanding wall described here has a *batter* (or lean) of 1:6, the universal standard. This means that for every 6 inches (15.2 cm) of height, the wall will taper in 1 inch (2.5 cm) for each side of the wall (that's 2 inches [5.1 cm] total). The height of this wall (4 feet [1.2 m]), minus the foundation, cover course, and coping stones is 3 feet (.9 m). With 36 inches (.9 m) of height, there are six 6-inch (15.2 cm) increments, meaning the wall will decrease 12 inches (30.5 cm) in thickness from the bottom to the top (figure 3). Walls with a consistent thickness throughout can and have been built; however, a wall with battered sides will last longer, has more character, and uses less stone.

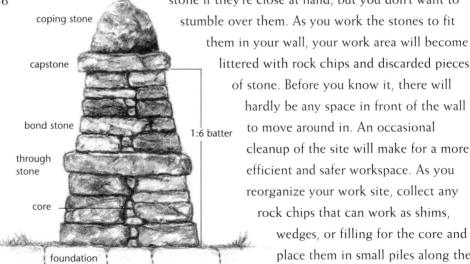

coping stone

capstone

bond stone

through stone

core

1:6 batter

foundation

Figure 3: Profile of a freestanding wall

SITE SETUP

This information will also be useful for any large project you undertake. An organized project site is more productive, more enjoyable to work in, and safer. Once your stones have been delivered, spend some time sorting them into piles of foundation stones, wall stones, and coping stones, dividing the material evenly along both sides of the wall's foundation area. Place the largest stones closest and along the length of the proposed wall. These will be used first in the foundation. The next largest pieces will be used for the courses of facing in the bottom half of the wall. Squared, blocky stones will be needed for wall heads or wall ends at both ends of the wall. Set long, rectangular stones around 30 inches (79.2 cm) long, in a separate pile to be used as through stones. Set capstones and thinner pieces for coping toward the back of the piles, because they'll be used last. Take this time to inventory your stones, and lay them out so you can see what you're working with before you start building.

Keep a path about 4 feet (1.2 m) wide between the wall and the piles of stone. It's easy to scan the piles of stone if they're close at hand, but you don't want to stumble over them. As you work the stones to fit them in your wall, your work area will become littered with rock chips and discarded pieces of stone. Before you know it, there will hardly be any space in front of the wall to move around in. An occasional cleanup of the site will make for a more efficient and safer workspace. As you reorganize your work site, collect any rock chips that can work as shims, wedges, or filling for the core and place them in small piles along the wall's foundation.

A typical freestanding farm wall in New England, U.S.A. Such walls can average 6 feet (1.8 m) in width at the base.

PREPARING THE FOUNDATION

A well-built, solid stone foundation is critical for the longevity of a freestanding stone wall. There are two ways of building the foundation: one with a perimeter that's even with the base of the wall, and the other with a perimeter that extends slightly beyond the wall's base. A projection of 2 to 4 inches (5.1 to 10.2 cm) will increase the foundation's strength and the overall stability of the wall. Extending the foundation beyond the wall's base is recommended for walls 4 feet (1.2 m) tall and taller (see figure 3 on page 45).

To mark off the foundation, drive two stakes in the ground at one end of the wall, marking the width of the foundation (in this case, 34 inches [86.4 cm]— that's allowing 4 inches [10.2 cm] extra on each side). Measure 24 feet (7.2 m) along the length of the foundation and drive the other two stakes into the ground

the same distance apart as the first two, leaving at least 6 inches (15.2 cm) of the stakes above ground.

Connect the stakes along the foundation's length with nylon string. Wrap the string around the stakes and pull it taut so that it's 3 to 5 inches (7.6 to 12.7 cm) above ground level. The area marked off should look like a long, narrow rectangle (figure 4). The general thickness of your foundation stones will determine the depth of the trench needed to set them in. When laid in the trench, the stones should be level with or slightly above the ground.

You need to lay the foundation on a firm, level, packed surface of soil. Remove any stones that project up through the soil and pack any holes with soil. Then compact any loose soil with a tamper. If you encounter rocks sunk in the ground that are too large to remove, clear the soil from around them until even

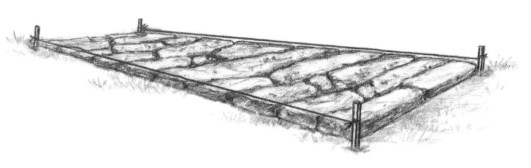

Figure 4: Foundation stones set to the height of string lines

with the base of your foundation trench. Then work the surface of the rock in with your foundation stone. Continue setting your stakes and string line and digging the foundation along the length of the proposed wall (if longer than 24 feet [7.2 m]).

LAYING THE FOUNDATION STONES

Choose the stones with the largest surface area and a minimum of 4- to 6-inch (10.2 to 15.2 cm) thickness (though make sure to save your longest stones for through stones). Start at one end of the foundation by laying your first stone with its length running toward the middle of the foundation. The foundation stones should extend from the outside edge into the middle of the foundation at least 12 to 15 inches (30.5 to 38.1 cm) (figure 4). Lay the most even side of the stone with its outside edge level with your string line. Set the outside edge of the stone as close to the string line as possible without touching it. If the stone touches the line, it'll cause the line to bow slightly, causing the foundation to do the same. You may have to dig down deeper to accommodate thicker stones or add more packed soil underneath thinner ones.

Any large voids beneath a foundation stone should be filled with as big a stone as you can fit into the void. Then wedge in smaller stones to completely fill the void.

Wedging beneath a foundation stone should only be done at the end of a stone that's set to the wall's center.

Lay the next foundation stone alongside the previous stone so the stones have as much contact as possible. If necessary, trim the stone to create a tighter fit. Continue setting foundation stones along both sides of the foundation. The overall surface of the completed foundation should be level from side to side and as even as possible.

Carefully fill any spaces left between the foundation stones with the largest stones that will fit in the voids. Then work in smaller stones and rock chips until every space is packed tightly. This process of filling the wall's core is called *hearting* and is often referred to as the soul of the wall. Packing the core is a deliberate and tedious process that will be done with each course in a freestanding wall.

THE WALL'S PROFILE

When building a new wall, "A" frames are needed at both ends of the wall's foundation. "A" frames outline the basic shape of a wall as it's viewed from the wall's end. String lines attached to the frames help gauge the height and width of each course as they taper inward. String lines are critical for keeping the wall's batter true from side to side and from the bottom to the top of the wall.

Building an "A" Frame

"A" frames can be made from wood or metal rods. For wooden frames, use 1 x 4 lumber for the uprights and cross members of the frames. You'll also need two pieces of rebar at least 5 feet (1.5 m) long.

For the 4-foot (1.2 m) high wall, cut two uprights (A) out of the 1 x 4, 40 inches (101.6 cm) long, which will leave a few extra inches at the top of the frame. There are three cross members. The bottom one (B) measures 29 inches, (73.7 cm), the middle one (C) measures 23 inches (58.4 cm), and the top one (D) measures 17 inches (43.2 cm) for a wall that's 2 feet (.6 m) thick at its base.

Lay the two upright pieces (A) out on an even surface. Space the pieces 26 inches (66 cm) apart (representing the width of the wall's base). Make sure the uprights are level, and attach cross member B to the bottom of each upright piece with a single nail on both ends of the cross member. Make a pencil mark at the center of the cross member.

Place one of the pieces of rebar in the center of the frame. (Use the pencil mark on the bottom cross member [B] as a guide.) Measure 3 feet (.9 m) up from the pencil mark and mark it on the piece of rebar with a piece of tape. Without moving the rebar, place a tape measure opened up to 14 inches (35.6 cm)

straight across the tape mark (with the rebar at the center of the measurement). Move the uprights until they meet both sides of the tape measure. This is where you'll attach the top cross member (D). Then attach the middle cross member (C) in the middle of the frame. Repeat for the second frame.

This frame will help your wall maintain the 26-inch (66 cm) base and help ensure your wall tapers to 14 inches (35.6 cm) at the top.

USING THE "A" FRAME

Stand one "A" frame on top of the foundaton at one end. Directly behind the frame, in the center, drive one of the rebar stakes at least 1 foot (.3 m) into the ground. To secure the frame in place, tie the frame to the stake (figure 5). With the 2-foot (.6 m) level set on the top of the frame, level it, which may require shimming underneath one of the legs. Repeat this at the opposite end, then set your string lines taut at the bottom cross members.

WALL ENDS (WALL HEADS)

While the wall tapers from the bottom to the top, the wall ends, also referred to as wall heads, are laid plumb. Wall heads are built with stout, squared corner stones that are locked together in a dovetail fashion from one course to the next. Laying single corner stones that are 6 inches (15.2 cm) thick provides the most stable wall end. Complete the wall end by filling in between the corner stones with smaller face stones. Plumb the wall end face stones as you build, using the 4-foot (1.2 m) level. If the stones' sur

Figure 5

faces are fairly rough, you'll have to take an average reading.

BOTTOM COURSES

Set the first course of the wall using the largest stones left after setting the foundation. Work along one side of the wall for 10 feet (3 m) or so, then work the opposite side. Set the stones parallel to the string line.

THE CENTER OF THE WALL

With each course, the center or heart of the wall will need to be packed solid with smaller stones and rock chips (figure 6). Packing the center tightly is critical for creating a sound wall. After the face stones on both sides have been set, you'll notice open spaces between them. Pack these empty spaces as you did with the foundation, using the largest rocks possible. Then, in the remaining spaces, set smaller rocks and pack rock chips into any voids between the stones until the core is filled as completely as possible. This is a time-consuming process that shouldn't be overlooked.

Figure 6: Small stones and rock chips are packed tightly in the voids between the foundation stones.

The core of this freestanding double-stone wall was carefully packed with smaller stones by students of the Dry Stone Conservancy in Lexington, Kentucky.

WEDGING

When needed, wedge underneath face stones at the interior of the wall. Avoid wedging stones along the outside face of a wall as much as possible. Walls may settle slightly over time, causing wedges to loosen and fall out, leaving the stone they were supporting with less support.

THE NEXT COURSES

Use the string lines as a general guide to match the top of each course You want to keep the course as close as you can to the height of the string line. Once you have packed the wall's core, you're ready to move the string lines up evenly another 6 inches (15.2 cm). Be sure to check that the string lines are taut and not sagging in the middle.

To avoid running joints (points of structural weakness), break the vertical joints between the stones of your previous course with the stones of the following course. The basic rule of thumb for any stonewall building is "one stone over two and two over one" (see figure 2 on page 45).

THROUGH STONES

Through stones, also referred to as ties, are set out on the course that is midway between the wall's base and the bottom of the capping. Place through stones in the course every 3 to 4 feet (.9 to 1.2 m), and break the joints of the course they're set on. Through stones that protrude beyond a wall's face by 3 to 4 inches (7.6 to

10.2 cm) provide more strength, and with the extra bit of stone revealed, they become a design element. Once they are laid out, fill in between them with face stones and hearting.

BOND STONES

The wall's upper half will narrow considerably, allowing only medium and smaller stones to be used here. It's preferable to have at least 6 to 8 inches (15.2 to 20.3 cm) of each stone extending into the wall for good contact. It's also preferable for long bonding stones to extend into and past the center. Bond stones extend horizontally into and beyond the wall center, binding the two faces of the wall together. Continue setting bond stones in the wall's upper courses. Alternate these stones from side to side to provide further strength to the wall. With bond stones that extend well past the center of the wall, consideration has to be given to the stone that will be set on the opposite side (the shorter stone has to have a minimum depth of 6 inches [15.2 cm]).

CHINKING

Chinking stones are small stones used to fill voids in the face of the wall. They're usually set in the wall as an afterthought. Sometimes I find a chink in a pile of scrap that works as is or it may need to be trimmed for a custom fit. The chink should fit far enough into the void so that it won't pop out. When setting a chink, you should be able to push the stone into the void and give it a light tap with the hammer for a snug fit without disturbing the stones around it. Avoid getting carried away with chinking. Sometimes when you step back and look at the total face of a wall, those small voids become shadows that seem to blend in just fine.

Through stones are placed in the course that's at the wall's halfway mark.

The Top of the Wall

Traditionally, this style of freestanding wall has a cover course of capstones with a course of coping stones stood vertically in a row on top of the capstones. You may choose to finish your freestanding wall with only a row of capstones and be happy with it. If you choose to cap the wall and leave off the coping, the capstones for this project should be about 3 inches (7.6 cm) thick and 16 inches (40.6 cm) long. Caps of this size completely span the upper surface and allow for a 1-inch (2.5 cm) overhang on each side.

CAPSTONES

Capstones help prevent rainwater from entering the wall's core, so tightly fit the caps together as you lay them. Single stones that completely span the upper surface from side to side are best. When fitting the caps, try to have a 1-inch (2.5 cm) overhang on each side of the wall. Level the caping by using wedges or shims underneath the stones. Making your final course of face stones as level as possible will make leveling the caps much easier.

COPING STONES

Coping stones are set on top of the capstones, if desired. They can be stood up completely vertical or with a 15° angle. If a wall is on a slope, the wall copes will slope downhill. These stones can be fairly thin, so it'll take a lot of them to complete the wall.

To start the coping, set a substantial, blocky, cube-shaped stone on top of the wall at one end. The first coping stone will fit snugly against this stone with the others following in a line, like books on a shelf. Coping can be done with single stones that span the width of the wall, in this case 14 inches (35.6 cm). Continue standing the stones to the opposite end of the wall,

A course of stout capstones secures the top of this freestanding, dry-stacked wall.

An even row of neatly stacked single coping stones tops a freestanding double-stone wall rebuilt with salvaged stone by the Dry Stone Conservancy.

where you'll need another blocky stone to hold the stones in place.

Set a string line to the average height of your taller coping stones and use the line as a guide. Some taller copes may need to be trimmed, while shorter ones will need to be shimmed.

To ensure that the stones don't topple off the wall, some of them may need wedges set at one or both of their outer edges. When all the stones are in place, fill in large gaps between the tops of the stones with thin wedge-shaped stones. Lightly tap them into place so they're snug.

DOUBLE COPES

Another style of coping is call *double copes*, where two smaller stones are set side by side on top of the capstones. Occasionally, the double copes will overlap slightly where they meet in the center. With double coping stones, it's good to insert a single coping stone every 4 feet (1.2 m) to strengthen the course.

Repairing Old Walls

One of the missions of the Dry Stone Conservancy in Lexington, Kentucky is to restore older rock fences and walls, many of which have fallen into disrepair because of neglect. Sometimes freestanding walls crumble because their core or center was not packed properly or the foundation stones have settled or shifted over time. Often, trees have been allowed to grow too close to a wall, and their roots cause foundation stones to shift.

While stripping out an old wall or just a section of one, observe the original builder's style, and look for reasons why the wall has deteriorated. The time spent separating the wall stones will be worth it when you go to rebuild the wall.

Start by removing the coping stones, placing them off to one side in a separate pile. Then remove the packing or hearting in the center of the wall first, and then remove the face stones. It might seem easier to just push the wall over, but then you'll have to separate stones from a jumbled pile. Continue removing the core and face stones, separating the material out evenly on both sides of the wall. When you rebuild the wall, you'll need material to work with from both sides.

When you get to the course with critical through stones, set them off in a separate pile. Remove all wall stones until you reach the foundation. Any foundation

This dry-stone wall will be stripped to the trench of its foundation as part of the restoration process.

stones that have moved or settled will need to be reset. If the foundation is in extremely poor condition, strip it out completely and start over.

Rebuilt with salvaged stone from old rock fences, this newly constructed fence was completed by the Dry Stone Conservancy. The wall's projecting foundation stones offer extra support. A row of single coping stones are stood on top of the capstones.

RETAINING WALLS

This dry-stacked retaining wall in Hunderton County, New Jersey is a striking landscape element. A slight curve in the wall shows off the tightly fit stonework.

WHEN YOU BUILD A STONE RETAINING WALL, you're creating a functional sculpture in the landscape—a permanent element of natural beauty in the garden.

Retaining walls are used to hold back earthen banks of soil. An exposed bank of subsoil is the result of cutting into the original grade of a slope. The exposed soil is vulnerable to gravity and hydrostatic pressure compounded by frost heaving in colder climates. These factors will eventually lead to various degrees of erosion if not contained. During the excavation of house sites and driveways in hilly and mountainous terrain, many areas are left with exposed banks that need to be retained. The soil in these situations is usually stable enough to hold up for awhile, but over time, the soil will crumble, particularly in wet climates. Dry-stacked retaining walls are constructed to stabilize these situations.

If built properly, a dry-stacked retaining wall will last as long as a mortared one and is cheaper and easier to build because you don't need a concrete footing and a block wall with an elaborate drainage system.

Building a Retaining Wall

These instructions are for walls that are 1 to 6 feet (.3 to 1.8 m) high. Walls built up to 4 feet (1.2 m) high are very common and make a reasonable project for the first-time wall builder.

CONSIDERATIONS

There are many similarities in the building techniques of dry-stone retaining walls and freestanding dry-stone walls. The main difference is that a freestanding wall has two wall faces and is self-supporting, while a single-stone retaining wall has one wall face and physically depends on the bank it's leaning into for support.

I build retaining walls with a single stone's thickness. I also tend to build with larger stone than most people would choose, particularly for walls over 3 feet (.9 m) tall. For this reason, later in this section I'll describe briefly how to stack a double dry-stone retaining wall using smaller stones while providing the necessary mass needed for a retaining wall to do its job.

The height of your retaining wall will depend on the height of the bank it will eventually protect. I've seen dry-stone retaining walls as high as 30 feet (9 m) that required an engineer's approval and highly skilled masons to build it.

You'll need to decide how thick the wall will be, whether it will be straight or curved, and whether the wall ends will taper, step down to the ground, or stand squared and level. Also, the height of your wall will help determine how thick it will be. A 2-foot (.6 m) wall, like the one shown below, is only around 20 inches (50.8 cm) thick, using stones that extend into the wall's interior from 4 to 18 inches (10.2 to 45.7 cm). The gravel backfill varies in thickness from 2 to 14 inches (5.1 to 35.6 cm), depending on how far a particular stone reaches into the wall. Taller walls, 4 to

The variety of stone sizes adds character to this retaining wall.

6 feet (1.2 to 1.8 m) high, are 24 to 30 inches (61 to 76.2 cm) thick (or thicker) because larger stones are used to make them more stable.

THE WALL'S BATTER

In order to be effective, a retaining wall needs to be built leaning back against the bank in order to prevent the soil from shifting (figure 7). Friction between the stones, the downward force of gravity, and the degree

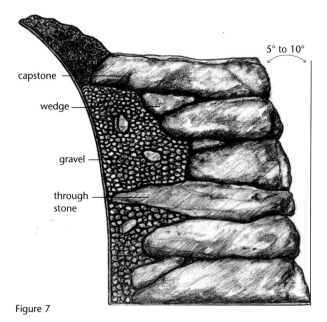

capstone

wedge

gravel

through
stone

5° to 10°

Figure 7

of lean or batter of the wall all combine to hold the stonework in place. A batter of 5° to 10° is fine for most walls 2 to 5 feet (.6 to 1.5 m) tall.

SELECTING STONE

The shapes and sizes of stone you want for building a retaining wall are similar to those in a freestanding wall (see page 43). If you've had several tons or more of stone delivered, sort them, taking a visual inventory as you do so. This will save you time and frustration when you're scanning the pile for a particular stone. You don't need to be too meticulous with the sorting; it's really a

matter of separating the largest pieces and then piling stones of similar shape and size together along the length of the wall to the outside of your working path.

• With retaining walls, the stones with the largest surfaces are used as capstones. Set them out of the way, because they'll be used last.

• The next biggest stones will be used as foundation stones. They can be set close to the wall site.

• Set the large, square, blocky stones near the wall ends.

• Long rectangular stones make good through stones for tying courses of stone and gravel backfill together.

• Finally, make sure you have gravel for your backfill, and you may also want to have several buckets filled with small shim and wedge stones. Shims and wedges can also be found among the scraps left from trimming and breaking stones.

SHAPING STONES

See page 44 for complete information on shaping stones for walls.

HOW MUCH STONE YOU'LL NEED

With single dry-stone retaining walls, 1 ton (.9 t) of stone equals approximately 30 to 35 face feet (9 to 10.5 m) of stonework, depending on the weight of the stone you're using. To calculate the amount of stone for your project, first determine the total amount of face footage of stonework in the wall. To do this, multiply the proposed wall's length by its height (including the wall ends). Then multiply the capstone's average depth in feet (usually 1½ feet [.45 m] or so) by the wall's length. Add the two figures together for the wall's face footage. For a conservative estimate, divide your total by 30 for the number of tons you'll need to find or order.

For example, if your wall is 20 feet (6 m) long and 3 feet (.9 m) tall, there will be 60 face feet (18 m) of vertical stonework along the front of the wall. Then, multiply the length by the capstone's average width in feet: 20 x 1½ = 30 face feet (9 m). Then, multiply the wall ends' width by their height (say 1½ feet [.45 m] x 3 feet [.9 m] = 4½ face feet [1.4 m] at each end). The total amount of face footage is 60 + 30 + 4½ + 4½ = 99 face feet, which you can round up to 100 face feet (30 m). Finally, 100 divided by 30 equals 3.3 tons (3 t). So you'll need approximately 3½ tons (3.15 t) of stone for your wall.

If your source for stone is not convenient to your site, I recommend adding an extra half ton of stone to your order for every 3 tons (2.7 t) ordered to ensure plenty of good stone to choose from. Often the preselected pallets of stone in wire baskets or those wrapped with plastic have good building stone but lack larger pieces to use as capstones. Consider buying a pallet of larger pieces for capping material or handpick them from the stone yard's random or select piles.

Wolf Atlerman of the Unturned Stone Company (Asheville, North Carolina) oversees the delivery of a tandem-axle dumptruck load of Virginia fieldstone.

HEIGHT AND WIDTH PROPORTIONS

The easiest walls to build are low "knee" or "bench" walls that are approximately 2 feet (.6 m) tall with an overall thickness of 18 to 20 inches (.46 to .51 m). Walls 4 feet (1.2 m) tall and taller should be a minimum of 2 feet (.6 m) thick. And although it's possible to dry-stack a wall more than 5 feet (1.5 m) tall, you have to use much bigger stones or build a double stone wall (see page 68).

SITE SETUP

See page 45 for basic site setup pointers. You'll need to decide where you want the face of the wall to be and cut back far enough into the slope you're attempting to retain to accommodate the thickness of the wall. For small projects or areas where heavy equipment isn't an option for the excavation, two people using a mattock, shovel, and wheelbarrow can move a lot of soil.

ANGLE OF REPOSE

The type of soil you're digging into will determine the angle of repose for the bank. (This is different from the wall's batter discussed on page 56.) The angle of repose is created when you prepare your site by digging out soil from the bank, while the batter is created as you build the wall.) For instance, the soil in a solid, undisturbed clay bank is dense and compacted, giving firm resistance to a retaining wall, so it can be cut back any-

The flat face of the boulder creates an impressive focal point in this quarried stone retaining wall.

where from 5° to 25°, angling from the bottom to the top. Soil that's sandy and loamy drains well, but offers less resistance, so the angle of repose should be less than 15°.

Dig down to undisturbed or load-bearing subsoil for the base of the wall to sit on. Don't build on top of fill soil unless it has settled for several years. Angle the cut in the bank from the bottom to the top and cut back any large roots that are exposed. The base of the cut where the wall will be built should have an even surface with a slight pitch of 5° back toward the bank. You don't need to dig a deep footing here; a slight depression of a couple of inches is plenty. This will be filled with pea gravel. Save any topsoil—it may be used along the back edge of the capstones at the top of the wall.

This photo addresses issues that need to be considered when preparing to build a dry-stone wall. Landscape fabric laid out over the bank after excavation keeps the clay subsoil separate from the wall's gravel interior. Sheets of plywood protect the concrete driveway's surface during wall construction. A single boulder is used at each end of the wall to secure and define the wall's ends.

present in the ground freezes and expands, pushing the soil up and outward. In these situations, the soil is often pushed into the wall's gravel backfill and continues moving through to the joints between the stones. If the soil is red clay, this can discolor the stone.

Spread the landscape fabric out against the bank allowing 1 foot

LANDSCAPE FABRIC

If you live in an area that experiences heavy frost heaving during the winter, you may wish to consider covering the exposed slope with landscape fabric before you begin building. Frost heaving happens when moisture

(.3 m) of it to cover the base of the cut and extend the rest to cover the exposed bank. To hold the fabric in place while working, pin it to the top of the bank with a series of nails (16 penny) or use rocks to weigh it down.

In regions where severe freezing causes the subsoil to expand, landscape fabric can be used to prevent the soil from pushing through the gravel backfill and into the joints between the stones.

GRAVEL AND STRAW

Spread a 2-inch (5.1 cm) layer of gravel out along the base of the cut in the bank as wide as the wall will be. If you're working around clay soil, you may want to extend the gravel out a few extra feet to keep you out of muddy soil if it rains. Another option to keep you from standing in potentially muddy soil is to spread out a thick layer of straw or hay along your working path in front of the wall.

A line of spray paint marks the front edge of a wall's base. The first course of stone is laid out in a row, with edges joined as closely as possible.

LAYING THE FOUNDATION STONES

The first course of stone will be the wall's foundation. These stones should be at least 3 inches (7.6 cm) thick and have the largest surface area (except for the capstones). You may need to use two stones to create a foundation that reaches all the way back to the bank. Start at one end, setting each stone on the gravel base with its top surface pitched slightly toward the bank, setting up the degree of batter the wall will need as it leans into the bank. Be careful not to pitch these or any other stones in the opposite direction (toward the wall's face).

Continue setting these stones, abutting each other as tightly as possible. Once you've laid about three-quarters of the foundation course, finish it off by working from the unfinished end of the wall toward the stones you've already set. Why do it this way? If you continue forward, you'll find yourself struggling to find just the right stone for the very last space, which at the wall's end, will be a visual focal point. It's easier to set the wall end stones first and then work backward. When necessary, fill in behind these stones with small ones to complete the width of the foundation. Pack underneath the edges of the foundation stones and in between them to create a solid, even surface.

THE WALL'S PROFILE

If you're building a particularly long wall that you want absolutely straight from end to end, consider setting a string line to work the first few courses of stone. To do this, set a stake (rebar works well) at each end of the wall in line with where you want the face of the wall. The stakes should be 3 feet (.9 m) long and set in the ground with 2 feet (.6 m) still showing. Drive stakes in the ground at each end of the wall, in line with where you want the face of the wall and set the string between the stakes several inches above the ground. As you lay the first course, set the face of each stone just behind the string line without the stone actually touching the line. When the first course is completed, move the string up each stake as needed and set the second course of stone, and so on. Once you have several courses set, you should be able to remove the string. From this point onward, check the wall's straightness while sighting down the length of the wall from one end.

CORNERS AND WALL ENDS

With each course, establish the wall's end first, and then either start laying the rest of the course from that point or work toward the wall end. Corners and wall ends are the most exposed and vulnerable spots in a wall, so they should be built with a good selection of squared and blocky stones. Stone mass is what you want, and the wall ends should be created with as few stones as possible. Corner and wall end stones need two faces that are 90° from each other (or at least close to that). A single boulder stone stood on end in line with the face of the wall is also an impressive way to establish the wall's end.

Rectangular pieces are ideal for corner stones. Alternate the length of their faces, as the corner is stacked in a dovetail joint design. Stones stacked in the wall's end that don't reach back to the bank will need another stone to fill the gap and make contact with the bank.

THE BOTTOM COURSES

Once the foundation course is completed, you're ready to start stacking another course of stone. At this point,

Corners and wall ends should have stones that fit well and offer a lot of mass.

Figure 8: Stone chips plug the gaps between stones in a course in order to prevent the backfill from spilling out.

pay close attention to the vertical joints between the stones in the foundation course, making sure that you break them with the next course. You don't have to start at one of the ends. Often, I'll stagger a number of my larger stones, setting them so they match up best to the foundation course. Fill in between these stones with medium and smaller stones, matching up to the height of the larger stones.

Each stone set in the face of the wall should have a slight pitch from front to back (or at least be level). Avoid setting any stone with its upper surface angled out toward the front of the wall. These stones are prone to slipping out of the wall, loosening the adjacent stones. Another way to achieve the batter in a wall is to step back each course of stone by about ½ inch (1.3 cm), which works best with stones of similar shape and size.

Some stones will butt up square to one another, making a tight joint between them. The gaps where the stones don't match up so well (leaving gaps for gravel to pass through) need to be plugged with rock chips. Set them back a couple of inches into the wall so they won't be visible. Filling the gaps is critical in

keeping the pea gravel backfill from spilling through the joints (figure 8).

BACKFILLING WITH GRAVEL

Once you have the second course in place with all the gaps plugged, you're ready to backfill with the gravel. If you have rubble stones (rounded irregular ones), use them to fill larger voids, mak-

Gravel backfill

Perennials spill over the tapered end of a dry-stacked boulder wall.

This series of impressive boulder walls steps down a steep slope to the waterfront along the southeast coast of Victoria Island, British Columbia.

ing sure their top surface is lower than the top edge of the wall stones. Fill any voids left with pea gravel up to the surface of the wall stones. Remember to pack the gravel, particularly along the back edges of the face stones.

Filling up the space between the stones and the bank with pea gravel (small crushed stone) is critical for a well-built wall. The gravel helps stabilize individual wall stones and provides critical drainage of rainwater.

In some situations, using gravel is less critical, such as when building low walls 1 foot (.3 m) or less in height, or when you're stepping each course of stone back dramatically so the face of the wall looks like a series of short steps. In these situations, it's fine to backfill with rock dust or soil. I prefer gravel instead of soil to backfill with because it's easier to pack around the stones and adds more stone mass to the wall.

Settle the gravel around the stones with a piece of rebar, a short crowbar, or the tapered end of a brick mason's hammer. Jab the tool into the gravel around the backs and sides of the wall stones, forcing the gravel into the voids. If, as you do this, the gravel disappears into a void beneath a stone, add more gravel or pull some forward from the backfilled area and continue setting it until the void is filled. Fill the gravel up to the top edge of the back of the stones you just set.

Before setting the next course, brush back any gravel remaining on top of the first-course stones; the first few inches of the top surface of every stone should be bare. Gravel on these upper front surfaces will prevent the next course from making good contact. Now you're ready for the next course of stone.

THE REST OF THE WALL

To complete the remaining courses, repeat the very same steps. As you work, keep the following tips in mind:

• To adjust the stones' angles, use wedge stones.

• If points or protrusions keep a particular stone from fitting well with the stone next to it, trim it for a better fit.

• If you have a difference in height between stones in a course, use smaller shim stones to make up the difference.

• Pay attention to the wall's batter as you work. After setting a couple of courses, stand at one end of the wall so that you're looking down its length. The slope of the wall should be 5° to 10°. If you don't know what a 5° batter looks like, imagine you're looking at a clock set at 12:05. The minute hand will rest at a 6° angle in relation to the hour hand.

• Remember to complete the last few feet of each course by setting the wall end stones first and then working backward, toward the stones you've already set.

• One of the keys to building a successful wall is creating tight joints by getting as much contact between stones as possible. Take your time choosing which stone to place down next. When a stone looks like it'll fit in a particular spot, place it there. Sometimes, by flipping the stone end over end, you may find it fits even better. If necessary, trim away protrusions or thin tapering edges to make stones fit more tightly.

• Add wedge stones (when needed) to stabilize a larger stone or a thin shim stone to adjust its overall height.

• Always keep the next course in mind as you lay the one beneath it. If a stone has major protrusions, that will present problems when you lay the next course. You may want to trim it or choose another one.

• Finally, avoid running joints—position your stones to cover the vertical joints between the stones in the course underneath. The rule of thumb here is "two stones over one, one over two, two over one," and so on. If the joints break in the same places, course after course, you'll end up with a running joint that will cause a weak spot, structurally and visually.

THROUGH STONES OR TIES

There are no strict guidelines for setting these particular stones. They are most useful in strengthening the wall after setting a number of smaller stones that don't reach back into the wall very far. Through stones can be long and rectangular, or they can also be long, wide, flat, thin stones similar to capstones, yet not thick enough to be a capstone. For a retaining wall, any stone that reaches well back into the wall's interior can be considered a through stone (see figure 7 on page 56).

This wall, made with quarried boulders weighing from 300 pounds (136 kg) to 2 tons (1.8 t) by master mason Jim Morris, tapers down with a series of stepped capping stones to meet a single boulder at the wall's end.

These courses of rounded glacial erratics are stepped back severely to create the wall's batter.

THE TOP OF THE WALL

There are three styles for finishing off the top of a dry-laid retaining wall. The top surface of the wall will be capped with capstones, which, in this case, are usually the largest stones with two fairly flat surfaces. If the bank of soil is the same height from one end of the wall to the other, then the surface of the capstones will be level from end to end. If, however, the soil bank gradually tapers downward at either end, the wall should do the same.

Stepped Wall

One way to taper a wall end is to construct it in "steps" by capping it off at varying heights. To build this way, you'll start at the lowest end of the bank, setting two or three courses of stone from one end of the wall to the other. Then, starting at the low end again, you'll begin setting capstones. When you reach the point at which the soil bank rises above the last capstone you've set, you'll stop setting capstones and stack another course or two along the remaining length of the wall. Then you'll set more capstones until the wall needs to step up again. Continue by repeating these steps until the wall's finished.

Tapered Wall

If the bank tapers at one or both ends, the graceful taper of the wall can be accentuated by allowing the capstones to follow that tapering line. This means the capstones will be sloped with the tapering end.

LAYING CAPSTONES

Properly set capstones are a protective course that prevents the wall stones from loosening. Setting the capstones can be tedious, time-consuming work, particularly if you want the wall to be level from end to end. If the finished wall is going to be 3 feet (.9 m) tall

These capstones are set at relatively the same height using the contour of the bank to determine the finished height of the wall.

and your capstones average 4 to 6 inches (10.2 to 15. cm) thick, start laying them when the courses of wall stone have reached 28 inches (71.1 cm) high. If you build up too high, you may have to take wall stones out in order to set the capstone at the correct height. The tedious part of capping comes from finding just the right stone or group of stones to fit underneath each capstone. It's easier to have a capstone selected and build up to match its thickness with the finished height of the wall.

If the wall's going to be level from one end to the other, you can start capping at either end. If the wall is

Set smaller capstones between and behind larger ones to conserve your supply of large stones.

stepped up with the grade of the bank, you'll need to start at the lowest end of the grade for the wall's end. Choose a capstone that also works as a wall end. Build the courses and wall end and set the capstone you've chosen. You may have to set one or two more at this level. Continue setting the wall ends, facing stones, and capstones until the grade steps up. Here you'll have to build another wall end and take the wall courses up at the same time. Continue stepping up until you reach the wall's finished height, and then set the remaining capstones level to the opposite end of the wall.

If you have a limited number of large capstones, consider staggering them and filling in between with the next largest stone. Once set, a capstone should be level along the length of the wall (unless it's at a tapering end) and have a slight slope to its surface from the wall's face back to the bank. Thoroughly pack underneath each capstone with pea gravel as your set them, then move on to the next one.

Large stones with only one flat surface can be used as capstones. Set the flat surface down on the upper course of wall stone so it has good contact. The other irregular surface will be the top of the wall. Capping with an irregular surface on top gives plenty of visual texture to the wall's upper surface.

Double Retaining Walls

Double dry-stone retaining walls are superior in strength to single stone ones and should be considered when building walls taller than 5 feet (1.5 m) or for securing extremely unstable banks of soil.

The profiles of a double dry-stone retaining wall and a freestanding stone wall (page 40) reveal many similarities. Use the directions given for building a dry-stacked freestanding wall for building a double-stone retaining wall, keeping the following considerations in mind:

• A double-stone retaining wall will use almost twice as much stone as a single-stone wall.

• Build up the interior and exterior courses at the same time and tie them together using bond and through stones.

• Only the exterior face is battered with a 1:6 slope from the base to the top; the interior wall is laid plumb (figure 9).

• Add backfill between the exposed bank and the interior wall as each course is completed.

• Cap the wall the same as a single-stone retaining wall.

Figure 9: Profile of a double-stone retaining wall

Repairing a Retaining Wall

My friends Barbara and Martin have a retaining wall that runs along two sides of their house. The wall appears to have been built well, but one 12-foot-long (3.6 m) section was seriously bowing with stones about to pop out. The clay soil used as backfill behind the wall would hold moisture, and when the ground froze in winter, bit by bit and year after year, it pushed a section of the wall outward.

My friends wanted the bowed section rebuilt, so I removed the stones down to a secure course at the bottom. With a shovel and mattock I cut the clay soil in the bank back, using a tarp to collect any soil that fell, making it easier to clean up the site in the end.

When I restacked the stones, I backfilled the wall stones with pea gravel and rubble stone, providing good drainage directly behind the wall. I set shelf stones in the corner of the wall that serve as steps to the top of the wall. With two people working, this was a half day's project.

Using clay soil instead of pea gravel as backfill caused this otherwise sound wall to bow.

BENCHES

BUILDING A FREESTANDING STONE BENCH can be as simple as finding three large stones that look good together. Another option is to build a low section of retaining wall that's capped off at a good bench height.

Freestanding Bench

Freestanding stone benches can be built just about anywhere and in a number of ways. A simple and common one is a rectangular slab of stone with a supporting stone set underneath at each end. A stone bench is a welcome site in a garden; its weathered surface has aesthetic appeal and is maintenance free. Stone benches are an invitation to sit and enjoy the surroundings, such as the sight and sounds of a creek or water feature, an open sunny spot in the garden, or the tranquillity of a peaceful private setting.

SELECTING STONE

The hardest part in building a freestanding bench will be finding a slab 3 to 5 feet (.9 to 1.5 m) long and the supporting stones. If you're not lucky enough to have an old piece of granite curbstone lying around, a

Large slabs of quarried stone were used to build this freestanding table.

trip to the stone yard may be in order. Don't count on finding exactly what you're looking for the first visit. Let people there know what you're looking for, and they may be willing to keep an eye out for you. Bench stones don't have to be rectangular in shape, but they

The backrest stone of this bench was sunk into an earthen socket dug well below ground level.

should be heavy and at least 2 inches (5.1 cm) thick. Triangular, rounded, and squared slabs of stone will also work, although they'll require three or four supports.

A bench stone should have a fairly even top surface, free of major protrusions that would be uncomfortable to sit on. If the bench stone's underside is also even,

it'll make better contact with the top of the support stones. For narrow rectangular benches, each of the two supporting stones should be blocky with enough surface area on one of their ends to amply cover the width of the slab. When three or more stones support a bench, it's less critical how much surface area comes into contact underneath the slab. Rounded stones with just a small point of contact work well when three or more support stones are used. The contact points of the stones will need to be of even height for the bench to sit level.

CALCULATING THE BENCH'S HEIGHT

The standard height for a bench is 17 inches (43.2 cm), so plan for your bench to be somewhere close to that figure. To calculate your materials, start by subtracting the thickness of the bench stone from the finished height of the bench, which will give you the height of the support stones from the ground up. Add the depth of the support stones set in the ground to the aboveground figure to get the total length of the support stones. For example, a bench stone that's 4 inches (10.2 cm) thick requires support stones 13 inches (33 cm) from the ground up. If the support stones are blocky and set 6 inches (15.2 cm) into the ground, they would need to be a total of 19 inches (48.3 cm) long.

SETTING THE SUPPORTS

Supporting stones that are blocky with a wide bottom won't need to be buried deep in the ground. Supports that are narrow slabs will need to be buried 12 to 18 inches (30.5 cm to 45.7 cm) in the ground, depending on the size of the bench (see figure 10 on page 72). Support stones that are slightly longer than needed can be buried a little deeper to get the necessary height. If the support stones have an even upper surface, they'll make better contact with the bottom of a bench stone.

Start the project by marking the holes for the support stones a reasonable distance apart (that fully supports the bench stone). I like to allow for some overhang of the bench stone at each end. Dig the two holes the necessary depth and set one of the stones at the proper height (make sure it's also plumb). To set the second stone, use a level with one end set on top of the first stone reaching over to the top of the second one. Set the stone at the correct height. Secure

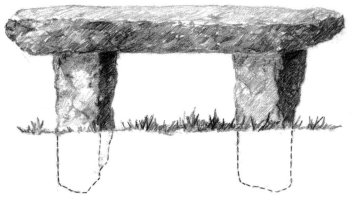

Figure 10: Narrow slab supports should be buried 12 to 18 inches (30.5 cm to 45.7 cm) in the ground.

the stones by filling in around them with pea gravel or soil, and compact the area with a tamper.

SETTING THE BENCH STONE

Help from a friend makes setting the heavy bench stone easier. If the slab is too heavy to lift manually, see page 149 for other options.

If your bench stone is heavier at one end than at the other, allow the lighter end to overlap its supporting stone by a greater length to make the bench appear more balanced. A bench stone that rocks even slightly is annoying, so take care to adjust this stone carefully on its supports. To find the best possible position, you may need to slide the bench stone back and forth across the supports until it's stable. A single well-fit wedge stone may secure a rocking bench stone.

If the bench feels high, you can spread some soil around in front of it. If it's too low, you can dig away some of the soil to custom fit the bench to the site.

You can also use two or three stacked stones as a bench support.

Dry-Laid Bench

If you'd like to try your hand at building a smaller "retaining wall" before moving on to a larger project, this bench is a good place to start. The bench shown below was part of a demonstration I gave at a public library. It took me about two hours to complete between setting up my materials to laying the bench-capstone on top. With a brick wall as the backdrop, I decided to build a small-scale retaining wall, cap it off with a single bench stone, and use the wall as a back-rest. The materials for the bench consisted of locally quarried building stone for the base, a piece of flagstone for the bench stone, and five 5-gallon (19 L) buckets of pea gravel. I used a wheelbarrow to move the pieces of stone and buckets of gravel from my truck to the library entrance.

Organizing your site is helpful when working on small-scale projects.

rim at the top for the bench stone to sit on. Once you've completed the base, have a friend help you lay down the bench stone.

CALCULATING THE BASE'S HEIGHT

The bench height was to be 18 inches (45.7 cm) when capped off with the bench stone. With a bench stone 2½ inches (6.4 cm) thick, I needed the base to be 15½ inches (39.4 cm) high. The base stones were fairly large ones, and I knew that the fewer stones I used on such a small project, the more solid the bench would be.

STACKING THE BENCH

Familiarize yourself with the dry-laid wall-building technique on pages 54 through 68. Begin by removing the grass and about 4 inches (10.2 cm) of topsoil. Fill the void with crushed stone and pack it with a tamper. Next, set the first course of stones, using the brick wall to hold in the gravel backfill.

Continue setting your courses, and stack your last course level so you'll have an even

BORDERS

FOR A VERY DELIBERATE and attractive looking border to surround a path, paved area, or garden bed, look for stones with two flat sides that are of a similar thickness when stood on their narrower edge. These stones should be twice the height of the finished border. For example, if you want 5 inches (12.7 cm) of stone revealed above ground, the stone should have 5 inches (12.7 cm) below ground for a height totaling 10 inches (25.4 cm).

This border was created with weathered pieces of sandstone.

Small, rough boulders create a raised bed for perennials and a Japanese maple at Warren Wilson College, Swannanoa, North Carolina.

Start at one end of the garden bed or path and dig a short length of trench wide enough to set the stones into. A shovel or posthole digger works well for this type of digging. Set the topsoil off to one side. The subsoil can be shoveled into a wheelbarrow and set out of the way.

Lay out six to eight stones, matching the ends that fit together well. Stand them up on edge in the trench and adjust their heights as needed using a level as a guide. Pour gravel or soil under the shorter ones. When the stones are set the way you want, fill in around their sides with the gravel or the topsoil, and pack the soil down with a tamper.

Round, irregular stones border this garden's perimeter. The ones in the center double as stepping stones.

Circular planting beds were created with a mix of large and small rubble stones. The larger stoness are set in a shallow trench; smaller stones are used to even out the height of the border.

STEPS

Sections of stone wall frame these steps. The stonework was locked together by building the steps first and then building the wall to meet them.

By choosing large stones of the same thickness, no riser stones were needed to build these steps. The dry-stone retaining walls lock the steps into place.

STEPS COMBINE FUNCTION AND BEAUTY in a way that makes them one of the most practical and visually inviting hardscape features in a landscape. A well-built set of steps works with the landscape, opening up areas that otherwise may not be accessible—each step offering its own vantage point for viewing a private garden or distant vista. The dry-laid method is the most practical way of building a series of steps, and stone will last longer than wood, brick, or concrete. You can design your steps to go straight up a slope, zigzag, or flow with elegant, serpentine curves. They can also be built directly into a dry-stone retaining wall, allowing easy access to an upper walkway or gardening beds.

Building Your Steps

If you have a steep bank, you may want to design the steps with a series of "S" curves or a combination of steps and paths that run perpendicular to the slope. A long series of steps going straight up a bank will be the most direct path, but it may be more interesting or practical to curve your steps.

Boulders help lock these steps into place.

The *riser* is the vertical front portion. In order for your steps to be easy to negotiate, the depth of the tread and height of the riser (known as the *rise*) should be fairly consistent from step to step. With single stone steps 6 to 8 inches (15.2 to 20.3 cm) thick, the rise is simply a part of that stone. With treads that are 2 to 4 inches (5.1 to 10.2 cm) thick, you'll need individual riser stones laid underneath the tread's nose to create a specific height.

With dry-laid steps, the weight and broad surface area of each tread stone help to stabilize the series of steps. Tread stones with a large surface area will have more contact with the bed of gravel beneath them, increasing their stability.

The relationship between riser and tread dimensions will vary from one set of steps to another. Steps on a long gradual slope, for example, may have fairly long treads and fairly short risers, while a steep slope may require short treads and tall risers. A good formula for determining a suitable tread depth and rise is: (Rise x 2) + tread depth = 26 inches (66 cm). For example, if you want a 5-inch-tall (12.7 cm) riser, your tread depth should be 16 inches (40.6 cm).

STEP HEIGHT

A step height between 6 and 8 inches (15.2 and 20.3 cm) works well for most situations (the standard building code for indoor steps is 7¼ inches [18.4 cm]). Steps with a consistent height from one step to the next are more predictable, making them easier to use, particularly in low-light situations.

If you choose to angle your step up a slope, you'll need to retain the soil on one side of the steps. Depending on how deep you have to cut into the slope, single, blocky stones may do, or a low retaining wall of smaller stone may be appropriate. If you don't retain the exposed soil, you'll find soil spilling onto the tread surface. In addition to retaining any exposed slope, it's good to set chunky pieces of stone to either side of the front edge of the step to help physically and visually anchor the tread stone.

CONSIDERATIONS

The top surface of a step (the part you step on) is called the *tread*. The surface of the stones you choose should be fairly even and coarse, rather than smooth. An extremely smooth surface becomes slick and dangerous to walk on when wet. The front or leading edge of a tread is referred to as the *nose*.

LANDINGS

A landing is a level spot in a series of steps that is longer and generally wider than a single step. A landing provides space for two people to pass in a series of steps and may be a welcome spot for people to stop to catch their breath. It'll be easier to incorporate a landing in an area where the slope is less severe. The bottom landing can be the ground or the end of a path.

SELECTING STONE

Large, heavy pieces of stone work best for this type of project. Use a medium to dense stone, as soft stones will wear out too quickly. Sandstone works well for general use in most house and garden settings. Basalt, slate, gneiss, or quarried granite will also work. The granite steps up to the Capitol building in Washington, D.C., are used daily by thousands of people. With that type of daily use, granite is about the only stone that can hold up from one decade to the next. Granite, however, is extremely heavy and much harder to shape than other stones.

The flagstone used in the project on page 78 is light gray sandstone of medium density quarried along the Cumberland Plateau in Eastern Tennessee. In Pennsylvania, along the Delaware River, a similar stone is quarried and referred to as blue stone because it's blue-green in color. In the southwestern United States, flagstone comes in a variety of earth tones from brown and tan to pink and red.

It's common to find this type of stone precut for steps, paving, and mantels. Special orders are not unusual, but they can take four to six weeks for deliv-

Steps, a short pathway, and low walls transform a bank into a welcoming site. Low-level lighting makes the steps safe at night.

ery. This type of stone is sold by the square foot when cut to specific dimensions and by weight with more random shapes.

SHAPING STONES FOR STEPS

Shape your treads so they are comfortable to step on. Make sure they have broad surfaces with straight edges (noses). For curves, split treads with slight tapered edges that accommodate the curves.

STONE SIZE AND WEIGHT

You can reduce the surface area and weight of each tread stone by half and still have a fine set of steps. The piece of flagstone below is roughly 2 x 4 feet (.6 x 1.2 m) and weighs 150 to 180 pounds (68.1 to 81.7 kg). Smaller pieces 2 x 2 feet (.6 x .6 m) and weighing 80 to 100 pounds (36.3 to 45.4 kg) will do and are easy for one or two people to set in place. If you want a wide set of steps using the smaller pieces, place two or three tread stones side by side.

By breaking this large, fairly square slab of sandstone along a diagonal, two wedge-shaped tread stones were created.

HOW MUCH STONE YOU'LL NEED

How much stone you'll need depends on how many steps you want and the size of the treads (depth, width, and thickness).

SITE SETUP

Determining the rise and run of the area where the steps are to be built will also tell you how many steps you'll need. The horizontal distance from first to last step is called the run. This measurement is taken along an imaginary, level, horizontal line. The overall rise of a series of steps is a measurement taken along a plumb, vertical line.

If your steps are meeting up to a fixed point, such as a patio or a paved pathway, this measurement will be critical. On the other hand, if the spot where the steps begin and end is arbitrary, this measurement is less important. A minimum tread depth should be 14 inches (35.6 cm) with the riser height being between 4 and 8 inches (10.2 and 20.3 cm). The slope of the bank will give you clues for determining the tread depth and the rise of each step. A long, gently sloping bank will need longer treads and a shorter rise for each

The rise and run of this short series of steps had to be calculated before building to properly connect the fixed points at the top and bottom.

step, while an extremely steep bank will have more steps with shorter treads and taller risers.

The easiest way to measure the rise and run at your step site is with the help of a friend. You'll also need two 2 x 4s (one at least 8 feet [2.4 m] long and one about 4 feet [1.2 m] long), a 2- to 4-foot (.6 to 1.2 m) level, a measuring tape, a pencil, stakes, and a hammer.

To mark the ground where you'd like the top and bottom steps to be, set a stake at each location. Then give your friend the level, the shorter 2 x 4, and the pencil. At the bottom of the slope where you want the steps to begin (where you've placed the stake), pound

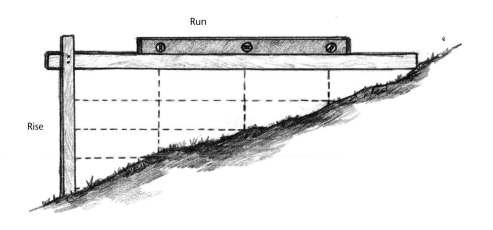

Figure 11

the shorter 2 x 4 in the ground (cut a "V" point at one end to make this easier). Check the 2 x 4 for plumb with the level.

Take the longer 2 x 4 and position it horizontally, with the free end sitting on the slope and the other end held flush against the vertically set 2 x 4. Check its position with the level. The two 2 x 4s should meet at a 90° angle. The lower edge of the horizontal 2 x 4 represents the run of the steps; the inner edge of the vertical 2 x 4 represents the rise (figure 11).

Next, have your friend make a pencil mark on each 2 x 4 at the inside corner where the two pieces of lumber meet. After making these marks, place the 2 x 4s on the ground and measure the marked distance on each one. These two measurements constitute the rise and run of your future steps.

After calculating the rise and run of the slope, you can use the results to come up with the tread depths and riser heights to suit your site. For example, if the run of your site is 6 feet (1.8 m) and you'd like to have four steps, divide 6 by 4 to get the depth of each tread—in this case, 18 inches (45.7 cm). To calculate the rise of each step, divide the overall rise of the slope by 4. For example, if the rise is 24 inches

(61 cm), and you have four steps, divide 24 by 4 to get the rise of each step—in this case, 6 inches (10.2 cm). Since we're working with stone, the rise and run may not be exact each time. When you're building the steps, try to stay within ½ inch (1.3 cm) of your riser and 1 inch (2.5 cm) on your estimated tread dimension.

LONG SLOPES

If the slope you're working with is long, you may have to take two or more readings to get the total rise and run. If the free end of the longer board sits only halfway up the slope, you'll need to reset the upright stake and take another measurement. If the free end of the longer board is positioned at the top of the slope, you can figure your total rise and run at this point. To take more than one measurement you'll set a separate stake at the point where the free end of the longer board is positioned and then reset the board to take another measurement.

THE LANDING TREAD

Once you have determined the step's rise and run, you're ready to get started. Set up the site with the treads, riser stones, and a pile of pea gravel close by. Starting at the bottom, use a mattock and shovel to dig out an area large enough to accommodate the first tread stone. The top of this stone will sit level with the ground and is more of a landing than a step. Dig deep enough to include a 2-inch (5.1 cm) base of pea gravel and the thickness of the stone. You don't have to include a landing tread in your design if you wish the ground to be the landing.

LAYING TREAD STONES

The tread surface of each step can be made up of one stone or several set in a line. Always begin your steps at the bottom of the slope. Set the first tread stone or stones using a 2- to 4-foot (.6 to 1.2 cm) level. Check the surface for level from side to side. Use a small plumber's level to check the tread from its back edge out to the front, which should be level or have a slight pitch (toward the front edge) of no more than $\frac{1}{8}$ inch (3 mm) to ensure that rainwater runs off.

Digging into the bank for the next step

SETTING THE RISER STONES

Use the mattock and shovel to dig back to your mark in the bank and remove the soil downward to the top of the stone's surface you just set. Now you can set the riser stones that will support the next tread stone. Set these stones with their faces on the line you drew earlier.

To determine the height of the riser stones needed, subtract the tread stone's thickness from the individual step height. The difference is the height of the riser stones.

After setting the riser stones, lower the tread stone into place with its front edge (the nose) overhanging the riser stones by about 1 inch (2.5 cm). The packed gravel bed offers a solid, well-drained surface for the back of the tread to rest on securely.

Now you're ready to dig a shelf into the slope to accommodate the next step. Decide where this step will be located according to your design. And with a straightedge and pencil, draw a line where the next risers will be set to support the next tread. Measure the depth of the next tread stone from this line into the slope. This determines how far back to dig into the bank.

Small pieces of select stone are carefully stacked and leveled to construct the risers.

Setting the landing level with the ground offers support for the first risers.

Exposed areas along the sides of the steps need to be plugged with stones in order to retain the gravel backfill.

Risers can be made up of one single stone, if you have the right one, or by combining a number of smaller stones. For setting a number of smaller ones, find two that are the height you determined the riser needed to be. Set one of these at each end of the line you marked on the tread's surface. Lay the 4-foot (1.2 m) level across these two stones and fill in between them with other stones, using the level as a gauge to build up to. At each end of the riser stones, more stones will need to be set perpendicular to these going back into the bank. These stones help contain the gravel you'll be pouring to fill in the area behind the riser stones.

POURING THE GRAVEL

Working from behind the stones, use rock chips to fill any gaps between the riser stones that are large enough for gravel to spill through. Fill the area directly behind the risers with pea gravel and tamp it lightly without disturbing the riser stones (figure 12). The gravel should be level with the upper surface of the riser stones that contain it.

Figure 12: Packed gravel supports the tread stone.

SETTING THE NEXT TREAD STONE

Ideally the tread stone should be set down on top of the risers and gravel bed with a great deal of control without disturbing the stonework below. For setting large tread stones, you may want to enlist the help of a friend. By standing the stone on one edge of the poured gravel, you can then gently lower it down with the front edge set on top of the risers. With the tread stone in place, make sure it's level from side to side and that it has a slight pitch toward the front.

Continue setting your risers and treads this way until you reach the top of the series of steps. If you're setting two or more tread stones together to form one step, be sure that their front faces match well and the stones are set together as tightly as possible.

BUILDING STEPS INTO A WALL

To build steps into a wall, figure exactly where you want them to be positioned before you start laying the wall's foundation course. Often a series of steps looks more interesting when it starts out wider at the bottom and narrows slightly as the steps reach the top.

Integrate the stone steps with the retaining wall by building the two elements at the same time. Refer to page 54 for more information on retaining walls.

When you're at the point of laying out the wall's foundation, make the steps the priority by setting your landing stone(s) and first step. Then set the wall's foundation course and any additional courses needed to meet up level with the surface of the first tread. Set cornerstones and wall ends on both sides of the step's opening.

Backfill behind the wall's first course, set your next step, and then continue bringing the wall up even with the surface of the second step. Once the second step is set, you'll see that the steps are passing through the wall. Set wall end stones running perpendicular to the length of the wall's face so they run back into the bank of soil. The stonework at the wall end will be capped off and stepped upward along with the treads and risers.

A narrow set of steps is easily built into this dry-stacked retaining wall of lichen-covered stones.

PAVING

Three-inch-thick (7.6 cm) sandstone pavers are dry laid in a bed of pea gravel.

WITH DRY-LAID PAVING PROJECTS you won't have the extra expense of concrete and mortar. A good selection of stone set on a gravel base makes a durable attractive surface ready for years of enjoyment. Those bare spots of ground around the house that get a lot of foot traffic are perfect for a paving project. You could create a simple stone path to cover those dozen steps made so often to the recycling bins and trashcans. Or you could pave a landing at the bottom of the steps off the deck or the stoop at the back door. A larger-scale project might be a dry-laid patio.

Paving Your Site

These project instructions can be used for any variety of paving project you have in mind.

CONSIDERATIONS

With any paving project the drainage of the area is an important consideration. You don't want your project to end up under standing water or for your basement to flood. This is most critical for paved areas with a large surface area, particularly ones that abut a building's foundation. Redirecting rainwater and improving a site's drainage will be discussed further on page 87.

To protect the siding of your home from rainwater splash, the tops of any stone next to a building should be at least 6 inches (15.2 cm) below the siding. Determine the average thickness of your pavers and add 4 inches (10.2 cm) for a base of gravel the stones will be set on to figure how many inches of soil you'll need to remove. If it's not possible to achieve the 6-inch (15.2 cm) distance between pavers and siding, then consider setting the pavers out from the foundation at least 6 inches (15.2 cm).

SELECTING STONE

Paving stones need one surface that's fairly even and coarse (for good traction). They also need to be of a thickness relative to the size of its surface area. For dry-laid paving, stones with a small surface area of 6 square inches (39 cm²) and smaller (used to fill in between larger stones) will need a thickness of at least 6 inches (15.2 cm) to be set securely in a base of pea gravel or rock dust. Stones with a surface area of 6 to 12 square inches (39 cm² to 78 cm²) should have a minimum thickness of 4 inches (10.2 cm). Pavers with surface areas 1½ square feet (117 cm²) and larger can have a minimum thickness of 2 inches (5.1 cm).

Stones with edges that are squared rather than sloped or tapered are best. Often, a tapered surface can be easily trimmed with a hammer. If you're paving with fieldstone or random quarried stone, the stones' thicknesses can vary quite a bit. If paving with stones of a more uniform size, choose pieces of cut flagstone that measure 2 to 3 inches (5.1 to 7.6 cm) thick and 1½ square feet (117 cm²) or larger.

Avoid using stones with smooth surfaces, such as polished granite or marble. Stones that are extremely soft should be skipped over as well; they won't hold up to much wear and are likely to flake off and become a nuisance.

HOW MUCH STONE YOU'LL NEED

Figuring the amount of stone needed depends largely upon the average thickness of the stone. Large slabs of random or cut sandstone, 3 inches (7.6 cm) thick, will pave roughly 75 square feet (6.8 m²) per ton (.9 t). With pieces of field or quarried stone averaging 4 to 6 inches (10.2 to 15.2 cm) thick, 1 ton (.9 t) will pave 40 to 50 square feet (3.6 to 4.5 m²).

SITE SETUP

After determining how deep you have to dig to keep rainwater from affecting a standing structure, such as a home, your next steps are to stake out the pad's perimeter and determine the pitch of your project area.

STAKING OUT THE PAD'S PERIMETER

If you have a general area that you'd like paved, draw a design that'll work with the location, then mark it on the ground. For laying out square and rectangular shapes, use wooden stakes and string line. For more organic shapes, use a garden hose, sprinkle corn meal, or spray paint. For pads that abut a foundation wall, use the wall to help you figure out the perimeter of a square or rectangular area.

If your site features straight edges, use a tape measure to plot its exact position, then mark the perimeter with stakes and string. To square up the corners, apply

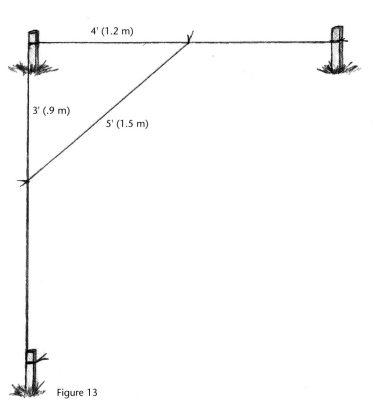

4' (1.2 m)

3' (.9 m)

5' (1.5 m)

Figure 13

a bit of basic geometry known as the triangle method: measure 3 feet (.9 m) along one leg of the triangle formed by the corner and mark that point; measure 4 feet (1.2 m) along the other leg of the triangle and mark that point; the diagonal between the two points will measure 5 feet (1.5 m) if the corner is square (figure 13).

If you need to mark a precise, circular shape, use a stake and string as a compass, and place stakes at 1-foot (.3 m) intervals along the resulting arc.

After outlining your floor, use the rope, hose, or string lines as guides and mark the ground with powdered chalk, lime, sand, or marking paint.

DETERMINING THE PITCH

A paving site next to a building must be pitched (or sloped) so that water will run down and away from the building foundation. The standard pitch for dry-laid paving projects is $\frac{1}{4}$ inch (6 mm) per linear foot (30 cm) of paving (2-percent slope). You can create a pitch as little as $\frac{1}{8}$ inch (3 mm), which is a 1-percent slope, but don't create one larger than $\frac{1}{4}$ inch [6 mm]. This means that for every foot of paving, measured from the highest point of the site to the lowest, the paved surface must slope from $\frac{1}{8}$ to $\frac{1}{4}$ inch (3 to 6 mm) downward. This slope's nearly imperceptible to the eye (not to mention the feet), but it's just enough to direct water flow.

To calculate the overall pitch for your site, measure the distance from the edge of the site that should be the highest, to the outermost edge of the site, running your tape measure in the desired direction of water flow.

Now multiply that length in feet by $\frac{1}{4}$ to get the inches of pitch needed. If, for example, your site measures 8 feet (2.4 m) multiply $\frac{1}{4}$ by 8. The result, 2 inches (5.1 cm), is the required pitch. The soil at your site must be 2 inches (5.1 cm) higher at the beginning than it is at the far edge.

REMOVING THE SOD

If you're planning to pave a large area, such as a patio or a path, you may want to rent a gas-powered sod cutter that removes sod mechanically. For smaller areas, you can use a manually operated sod remover or a digging spade with a square blade.

GRADING THE SITE

To create the correct pitch for your site, you'll probably need to add or remove soil from some areas. Use a mattock and a squared-edged shovel to remove soil. To build up the soil, first add a layer of damp subsoil (damp soil is easier to compact) or road bond, 3 inches (7.6 cm) thick. Tamp the soil down well and repeat the process, adding subsoil in layers, until the desired height is achieved. Stand at the outermost edge of the site and kneel or lie down so that your eyes are at ground level. From that vantage point, you should be able to see a slight incline all the way up to the highest point.

A more accurate way to monitor the pitch is to use a level—a 4-foot-long (1.2 m) model works best. First,

set the level on any level surface. Then place it so that one end sits at the high end of your site (for best results, lay an 8-foot (2.4 m) 2 x 4 in the trench and lay the level down on top of it). When the ground is sloping 2-percent, the level's air bubble will rest against the outer line on the level's vial (figure 14). As you grade (working your way down the site's slope), periodically rest the level on the ground and adjust the soil, as necessary, to achieve your 2-percent slope. (Make sure when you set your level down on the soil or pavers that it's pointing in the right direction, or you'll end up with the pitch directed toward the foundation instead of away from it.)

OTHER PITCH AND GRADING CONSIDERATIONS

• The pitch of a site not adjacent to a building is less critical, but a slight pitch is still desirable to reduce the chance of standing water.
• Compacted clay soil or packed road bond work well as the base for dry-laid paving. With a properly pitched site, rainwater will pass through the gravel beneath the stones and follow the slope. Loamy, spongy soil doesn't provide the best support for stone paving. I've watched stones sink into spongy topsoil over a relatively short period. Consider removing this soil down to the subsoil and then build back up with tamped layers of clay soil or road bond to the point that will give you the correct height with the pea gravel and paving stones.
• The best way to determine how well rainwater drains from a site is to get out there when it's raining.

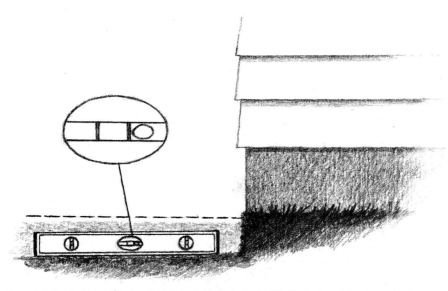

Figure 14: The bubble in the level's vial should look similar to this illustration, if the ground below the pavers has been pitched properly.

This is particularly useful after you've graded your site and before you start setting the paving stones. If the rainwater runoff is considerable and concentrated in one area, you may need to capture it and redirect it to an appropriate area, which may involve installing a French drain, a dry streambed, or buried drainpipe.

• A 4-inch (10.2 cm) perforated drainpipe buried along the lower end of the paved area is the simplest way to capture and redirect rainwater. The pipe should be buried in a 6-inch-deep (15.2 cm) trench running parallel to the lower end of the paving. The pipe will have a series of slots in its upper half. Be sure the slotted half is positioned on top and wrap the pipe with filter cloth to keep sediment from clogging the slots. The drainpipe can be covered over with the gravel base and the final row of paving stone.

• The simplest form of a French drain is an 8- to 10-inch-wide (20.3 to 25.4 cm) trench dug in subsoil that's then filled with gravel. You'll make the trench deeper the closer it gets to where the water will exit, providing a constant dip to keep the rainwater moving. Use 1-inch (2.5 cm) gravel to fill the trench, allowing more space for the water to filter through quickly. This design works well in areas where there isn't continuous silt and broken-down leaf debris settling into the gravel.

SPREADING THE GRAVEL BED

Once you have dug out your site and it's properly graded, spread a 2- to 4-inch (5.1 to 10.2 cm) base of pea gravel. The gravel helps define the site visually as you work. It will also keep the site from turning into a mud bath if it rains. Finally, the gravel also helps water to drain away, and it makes it easier to adjust the pitch of each paving stone.

SETTING BORDERS AROUND PITCHED SITES

Unless the lowest edge of a pitched paving site has a border, the gravel at the outer edge will migrate in the direction the slope. You can either set your borders before spreading the gravel, or, if it isn't critical to you exactly where the borders are situated, you may set them when you're working with the pavers at the outer edge of the site. Here are some border ideas:

Flagstone pavers are laid out on a bed of pea gravel. A 4-foot (1.2 m) level is used with a length of 2 x 4 to check the paving's pitch.

• If the ground just beyond the low edge of your site slopes steeply, a low, dry-stacked retaining wall at the edge of the paved area makes an excellent border. Construct the wall so the pavers along the rim of the site also serve as the wall's capstones.

• Block-shaped chunks of stone make good borders. Sink them into the soil at the rim of the paving site and cap them with the outermost pavers, or, to add more definition to the rim, choose border stones tall enough to rise above the paved surface. You may need to fill the gaps in the vertical joints between the stones by inserting chinking stones, or gravel will leak from between the border.

• Squared timbers, anchored with lengths of rebar, make visually pleasing borders for sites with straight edges. These should be set on 2-inch-thick (5.1 cm) gravel beds placed along the site's exterior edges. The pavers should meet their interior edges. Start by digging trenches around the site, making them deep enough to hold both the layer of gravel and the timbers. Then drill ½-inch-diameter (1.3 cm) holes through each timber, spacing the holes 2 to 3 feet (.6 to .9 m) apart. Spread the gravel in the trenches and position the drilled timbers on the gravel. Then drive 2-foot (.6 m) lengths of ½-inch-diameter (1.3 cm) rebar through each hole and into the ground beneath the layer of gravel. You may either set the lengths of rebar flush with the tops of the timbers, or sink them and plug the holes with wooden plugs. Precut 2-and 4-foot (.6 and 1.2 m) lengths of rebar are available at home improvement centers.

SETTING BORDERS AROUND LEVEL SITES

Gravel won't migrate from a freestanding paved area that's flat and level, but a border will help define the site visually. If the border material doesn't have too many joints, it will also help discourage surrounding vegetation from creeping into the paved area.

Suitable border materials for level sites include long, squared timbers, lengths of steel edging, stone slabs stood on end, bricks, and Belgian blocks. Set their upper surfaces at or just above the paved area.

LAYING THE STONES

Start by laying out half a dozen paving stones along the upper end of the slope. If your paving site meets an inside corner where two foundation walls or a wall and outdoor steps meet, set the first paver in the 90° corner. If you wait until you've set the surrounding stones, you'll have to search for a cornerstone that is just the right size to fit a defined space. Trim the stones as needed to fit, with the joints between them averaging 1 inch (2.5 cm). Starting at one corner, set the first stone's surface at the correct height and angle for the desired slope. Be sure that this first stone is set correctly—you'll be using it as a benchmark for setting the rest of the paving.

To set the next stone, adjust its height by eye, adding or removing pea gravel. Lay your 4-foot (1.2 m) level across the first paver, with it extending to the edge of the second paver. This will indicate if the stone needs further adjustment in height. Place the level across the second stone to level it and adjust its pitch with the slope. For a final check, place the level across the two stones to see how they match up.

Continue to set the stone paving across this first row you have laid out. Where two stones meet, you may need to trim a section from one or both of them in order to make a tighter joint. With medium-density, 2- to 3-inch-thick (5.1 to 7.6 cm) flagstone, trim small sections off with a hand-set chisel and a 2-pound (.9 kg) hammer. For removing larger sections, you may want to score the stone using a cut-off or circular saw

A 4-foot (1.2 m) retaining wall alongside the outside edge of the steps and patio was built to retain the compacted soil and gravel needed to pitch the paving.

and masonry blade and then fracture the stone where it's scored with a hammer and chisel (see page 80).

Each stone will take a certain amount of attention to set it correctly. For stones with an uneven surface you'll have to take an average reading with the level or rely on sighting by eye. Be sure to pack gravel or rock dust around the edges of each paver as you set it. Avoid walking across the pavers you've already laid out and leveled but haven't completely set. If you have to stand on pavers that aren't completely set, stand in the middle of the larger ones and recheck them with the level before you move on.

Use a straight 10-foot-long (3 m) 2 x 4 to gauge the overall evenness of the paving. To do this, lay the board on its narrow edge across the paved surface, and while crouched down, look for low and high spots where the outside edges of the stones meet at the joints. If the edge of a stone is low, you may need to pry it up slightly, packing more gravel beneath it. If an edge needs to come down, dig the gravel out from between the joint at that point and try stomping down with your foot on the high edge of the stone.

FILLING THE JOINTS

Using a piece of metal rod (rebar) or a long narrow chisel, work the joints between the stones settling in the gravel. Tap on the rod or chisel with a hammer as you move along the joint, causing the gravel to vibrate and settle. You'll find spots where the gravel seems to keep disappearing as you tap the chisel; keep adding gravel until it levels off. Settle the gravel in the joints a good $\frac{1}{2}$ inch (1.3 cm) below the paving surface to keep from kicking the gravel out onto the paved area. Settling the gravel is tedious work that's necessary to fully support and secure the stone paving.

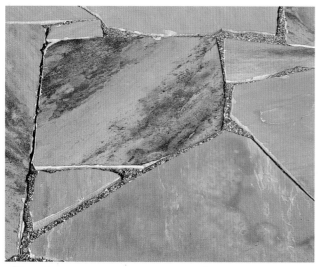

To create a deliberate pattern, these pieces of sandstone were shaped by scoring and cutting away unwanted sections.

Continue laying sections of paving, setting them and filling in the joints as you work toward the opposite edge from where you started. As you work toward hardscape features in the paving area such as tree wells, stone benches, and borders, lay out the paving next to them first before you get to them. It will be easier to work up to these areas with the paving directly surrounding them already laid out.

ROCK DUST

If you're using rock dust (quarry screenings) or coarse sand to set the stones, the process is similar. Use a tamper to pack the rock dust before setting the paver in its final position. To fill in between the joints, set a shovel full of rock dust on a paver, then use a brush to spread it around, filling in the joints. Pack the rock dust using something with a blunt edge, such as the rounded end of a chisel's handle or a scrap piece of 1 x 2 wood trim. A low, steady stream of water from a hose will further settle the rock dust into the joints. Whatever you fill the joints with needs to be at least $\frac{1}{2}$ inch (1.3 cm) below the paved surface. After the stones have dried, sweep any remaining rock dust into the joints.

JOINT FILLING OPTIONS

The gravel I've described for using with this paving project is crushed quarried stone that has the look of raw crushed stone. If that look doesn't appeal to you,

Moss works well for finishing off joints that have been filled with soil or rock dust.

use the crushed stone for the base and fill the vertical joints with a worn and more rounded gravel.

Another option is to allow for pockets of planting soil between the joints (particularly in the larger ones). In these areas, you'll remove the gravel at the base and fill the gap completely with amended soil and water-absorbing gel flakes that are available at nurseries. Eventually the plants' roots will reach the base soil. Until they do, the gel flakes help the soil retain moisture. Plant low, creeping plants in areas that get the most foot traffic and slightly taller plants in areas that are used less often.

Weed seeds are likely to fall into the joints of dry-laid paving. They will even take root in gravel. Anything you can do to encourage desirable, low-growing vegetation will reduce the amount of weeding necessary. Moss works best on top of the finer materials, such as river sand and quarry screenings. Experiment with several varieties of moss to see which take hold and thrive.

Regardless of what you do, some weed seeds will sprout anyway. If you take a few minutes every couple of weeks during the growing seasons, you can pluck them out easily just after they have sprouted.

The flat, even surfaces of this randomly set flagging serve more as stepping stones separated by grass.

Chapter 4

MORTARED STONEWORK

In the first few chapters of this book, you've learned about different types of stone, the tools used in stone-masonry, and building techniques for dry-laid stonework. If you already have a project under way, then you've also gained some valuable firsthand experience working with stone. This chapter on mortared stonework will open up new possibilities and many interesting options for using stone in the landscape, on the exterior of your house, and even inside your home. For those who are dedicated dry-stone enthusiasts, and others who may feel a bit intimidated by even the slightest mention of mortar, I hope this section will spark your interest, allay your fears, and empower you to give it a try.

BASICS AND TECHNIQUES

This cozy backyard includes a paved patio, a mortared bench wall, a fire ring, and dry-laid steps.

SO WHY BOTHER USING MORTAR TO SET STONE? Isn't it difficult? Honestly, I don't find mortared stonework any more difficult than dry-laid, though you do have to factor in mixing and using mortar, which admittedly can be a bit mysterious at first. There's no doubt that mortared stonework is different from dry-laid work, yet the two methods employ many similar techniques. One is not really better than the other; each has its place. For particular projects, mortared stonework is recom-mended, and sometimes required, such as stacking a stone veneer against a block retaining wall, using flag-stone paving on a concrete pad for a patio or walkway, or for building a hearth and fireplace, to mention a few.

This section isn't a complete catalog of everything you can accomplish with mortar and stone, but rather an in-depth look at the techniques used for setting stone in mortar, along with all the basic information you'll need for setting up your project site.

Concrete Footings and Pads

The biggest difference between dry-laid and mortared stonework is that mortared stonework is rigid and doesn't allow for the slightest bit of movement between stones. For this reason, a solid, concrete foundation is required in most mortared stoneworking projects (as well as in other masonry applications, such as brick and block work). A concrete foundation gives complete, unyielding support that's essential to maintain the integrity of the project. Vertical stonework, such as a veneered concrete block wall, requires footings (trenches) dug in the ground, that serve as a form for which to pour concrete. Concrete pads are created for mortared horizontal stonework such as a flagstone patio. It's the footings and pads that account for a bulk of the extra time and expense involved in mortared work.

There are some situations where concrete footings or pads won't be necessary. You won't need them in locations where the ground doesn't freeze. Also, if your project is relatively small, such as a 12- to 18-inch-high (30.5 to 45.7 cm) border wall, you could get away with a packed gravel footing. In all other situations, mortared stonework without a concrete foundation is likely to settle irregularly and be influenced by

A large concrete pad serves as a base for the patio, the fire circle, and the wall.

frost heave, which causes the mortar to crack, weakening the stonework and causing water damage and further deterioration. Many situations involving a concrete footing or pad will require the approval of your local building inspector, especially if you live in a city or suburban setting. This usually happens after the footers are dug or the formwork is set for a concrete pad and before the concrete is poured.

Concrete

Concrete is a thick, fluid mixture made up of gravel, sand, portland cement, and water. It's poured into footings that have been dug 1 to 3 feet (.3 to .9 m) below the ground's surface, depending on the frost line at a particular site. A concrete pad is poured onto a base of crushed stone and contained by constructed wooden forms. When the concrete sets up (cures), it provides a strong and uniform foundation on which to build.

ESTIMATING AMOUNTS OF CONCRETE FOR A PAD

The easiest and sometimes most efficient way to pour concrete is to order ready-mix that's delivered in a concrete truck. Generally, the smallest amount a concrete supplier will deliver is 1 yard (.9 m). To calculate the square footage of a square or rectangular pad, measure the length times the width in feet and the thickness in a fraction of a foot. In most cases, a concrete pad will be 4 inches (10.2 cm) thick, which is one-third of a foot (.33). If you're dealing with more organic shapes, measure as though you were working with a square or rectangle. This will give you a liberal amount of square footage, which can then be rounded off to a more conservative number before dividing by 27 to get the cubic yardage. (There are 27 cubic feet in a cubic yard, and 1 cubic yard equals .5 cubic meters.)

For example, if your patio is 12 feet (3.6 m) wide and 20 feet (6 m) long, those two figures multiplied together give you 240 square feet (22 m²) of surface area. Multiply 240 by .33 and you get approximately 80 cubic feet (2.3 m³), which equals approximately 3 cubic yards of concrete (divide 80 by 27).

ESTIMATING AMOUNTS OF CONCRETE FOR A FOOTING

Concrete footings need to be poured a minimum of 8 inches (20.3 cm) thick or two-thirds of a foot (.67). To measure amounts of concrete for footings, multiply the length by the width by .67, and follow the instructions above.

For example, a footer 2 feet (.6 m) wide multiplied by its length of 20 feet (6 m), gives you 40 square feet (3.6 m²). Multiply 40 by .67 to get 26.8 cubic feet (.8 m³). Divide 26.8 by 27 to convert cubic feet to cubic yards. You'll need approximately 1 yard (.9 m) of concrete.

POURING CONCRETE

If the concrete truck can't be positioned close to where the concrete will be poured, you have the option of moving it from the truck in a wheelbarrow. I strongly suggest having at least two wheelbarrows and three people available for pouring more than 1 yard (.9 m) of concrete.

Have your site completely ready for when the truck arrives. Plan a route for getting the truck right up to the project or as close as possible. The formwork and footings should be ready to receive the concrete before the truck arrives. Formwork is discussed in the projects' instructions.

Tools such as shovels, steel tooth rakes, trowels, striking boards, wooden floats, gloves, and rubber boots should be close at hand. Wet the site down in advance the day before if the weather has been dry. Concrete needs to cure slowly, and excessively dry sites will pull moisture out of the mix too quickly.

There's a limit to how much time you'll have when pouring concrete; things happen quickly once the concrete truck arrives. As the concrete is being poured for a slab, use shovels and steel-toothed rakes to spread it around. Once the form is topped off, you'll need to strike the concrete with a long 2 x 4 that's longer than the width of your form. Striking will knock down the high spots and even the surface out level with the top of your form.

To strike the pad, with the help of a partner, stretch the 2 x 4 along the top edge of the form. With short strokes, run the 2 x 4 from one end of the pad to the other, tapping or shimmying it along the form as you go. The vibrations created by the tapping help the concrete settle. At the same time, the 2 x 4 is helping you level the concrete as you move it across the form. At this point, you may have to add or remove concrete to achieve an even surface.

A freestanding, solid-stone wall separates a kitchen and family room. Granite cubes line the arched pass-through, and large slabs of stone strengthen the stonework and function as shelves.

Immediately after striking the surface smooth it with a bull or darby float. Then trowel the surface of the concrete. In this case, you'll be covering over the concrete with stone, so the finished concrete surface doesn't have to be perfectly smooth. Trowel the edges first, and as the concrete hardens, use pieces of plywood to kneel on as you work out into the center. Continue smoothing the surface until there's no water left.

Concrete footings and pads should cure a minimum of 24 hours before working on top of them. In extremely hot, dry weather, wet the surface of a concrete pad with a hose every two hours during the day once it has set up firm.

MIXING YOUR OWN CONCRETE

You can also mix your own concrete at the site, especially if you're working on a small patio or a short length of wall. Buy premixed concrete that comes in 40, 60, or 80-pound (18.2, 27.2, or 36.3 kg) bags. Read the specifics for the different types of premixed concrete: some are for footers that are load bearing, while others are "quick setting" and considerably more expensive. All you have to do is add water and mix with a mortar hoe in a wheelbarrow. Read the specific instructions on the bag. These premixed bags are certainly convenient and cost-effective for small jobs.

I've found that the standard concrete recipe works best with the projects in this book:

- 1 part portland cement (type 1)*
- 3 parts clean builder's sand**
- 4 parts gravel (crushed, washed stone from
  1/4 to 1 inch [6 mm to 2.5 cm])
- Water, clean enough to drink

The amount of water added to a batch of mortar will vary depending upon the sand's dampness. Once you've mixed a batch, you'll have a general idea of approximately how much water to add. Remember to add very small increments of water until the mix has the consistency of oatmeal.

*Portland cement (type I) comes in 47- and 94-pound (21.3 and 42.7 kg) bags.

**Builders sand is available at most building supply businesses and concrete block plants. This sand is sharp edged and finely graded. Always keep your sandpile completely covered with a tarp or large sheet of plastic when you're not working. Covering the sand pile will keep the sand dry and clean. Extremely wet sand is much harder to mix consistently with the other dry ingredients when mixing manually with a mortar hoe.

Start a batch by thoroughly mixing the sand and cement together using a mortar hoe, then work in enough water to make a thick, soupy mix. Add several shovels of gravel, mixing it in with the mortar hoe, then add several more, and mix. Continue until all the gravel's added. If the mixture gets too stiff to mix, add more water. It's best to use the concrete soon after the mixing is completed.

MORTAR

Mortar makes up about 10 to 20 percent of the total volume in a stone wall. Its function is to bond the stone and other masonry fasteners together. Mortar is similar to concrete, but it doesn't contain gravel and its consistency is quite different. Also, mason's lime is added to mortar to create a rich, sticky mixture. The material that brick and block masons use is quite porous, so the mortar they use is very wet, almost runny. Most stone worth using will be less porous than brick or block, so for the two styles of stonework described in this chapter, the mortar will be much stiffer.

TOOLS FOR MORTARING

A **mortar pan** or **wheelbarrow** is sufficient to mix mortar in for small jobs. I tend to work directly out of these, depending on how close I can get them to the stonework. If the stonework goes taller than 5 feet (1.5 m), and I start working on walk board and scaffolding, I use 5-gallon (19 L) buckets.

Two **mortar hoes** make the mixing go faster. A smaller mortar hoe with a 7-inch (17.8 cm) blade and two holes in it is easy to use. A larger hoe requires more strength to pull and is awkward to use if two people are mixing mortar together in a wheelbarrow.

For only one or two novice masons working on a mortared stone paving project, a wheelbarrow will do for mixing mortar. To keep your pile of sand clean, keep it covered.

A **square shovel** works best for shoveling sand and mortar mix and for scooping wet mortar out of the mixing pan.

I prefer a **medium-sized trowel** for placing mortar while setting stone, because it's easier to work the mortar in around the backside of the stonework. A **small buttering trowel** is handy for working mortar into tight spaces. If I need to place a large amount of mortar behind the stonework, I use a **shovel**.

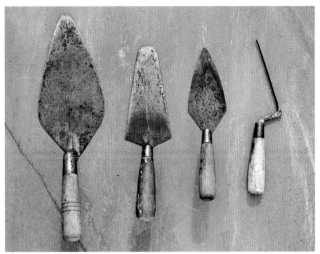

From left to right: a brick mason's trowel, a duckbill trowel, a pointing trowel, and a slicker trowel

MORTAR MIXES

As with concrete, premixed mortar is available and can be considered cost-effective for smaller jobs.

The standard mix for creating your own mortar is:
- 1 part portland cement (type 1)
- 1 part masonry cement (type S)
- 6 parts sand*
- Water

* You want sand particles that are coarse with sharp edges. For this reason, avoid using beach sand or play sand (meant for sandboxes). Both of these have rounded edges. River sand is fine if you can find it.

MASONRY CEMENT

There are many masonry cements available. Choose the cement that will fit your needs best, which in this case is type S. The exact ingredients and proportions in masonry cements usually are proprietary information.

Type M mortar is a durable mortar with high strength that's best used in foundations, stone veneer, and retaining walls. It can handle high compression loads.

IT'S IN THE BAG

At the building supply store, it's common for an employee to load bags of cement for you. Give him or her a hand if possible. Once you get a tear in a bag, it can be a mess, so if there's cement spilling out, refuse the bag. Also, only buy bags of cement mix from businesses that keep them in a covered, dry space. The bags should be somewhat pliable, so if you get a bag that's as hard as a rock that means it has gotten wet, set up, and is of no use. Even the moisture in the air can cause the bags to harden somewhat. For this reason, I hold off until all my other materials are on site before purchasing the cement mixture I need. Once the material is on site, it should be kept off the ground and completely covered with plastic.

Type S mortar has the ability to give when under pressure. It's good for stonework that will be subjected to normal compression loads. It has good adhesion, making this a good mortar for vertical veneer work and setting paving stones to a concrete pad.

Type N mortar is a general-purpose mortar for structures above grade such as masonry veneers and interior walls.

Type O mortar is for non-load bearing walls and exterior veneers that won't freeze if they get wet.

Portland cement-lime mortar is a durable mortar with a consistent hardening rate and a high compressive strength. The lime adds workability, water retention, and elasticity.

MIXING MORTAR MANUALLY

For most small projects, mixing mortar by hand is much more practical than renting a mortar mixer. A 6-cubic-foot (.18 m³) wheelbarrow is fairly inexpensive and easy to mix mortar in. Mortar pans come in several sizes. A small one 2½ x 5 feet (.8 x 1.5 m) will hold 6 cubic feet (.18 m³) of mortar and is a convenient size. Set the mortar pan close to the sandpile or near your building site. I usually set the pan up with a concrete block underneath each corner to reduce some of the bending when mixing.

Regardless of what method you choose for mixing the mortar, it's best to keep your sand and mortar mix materials in the same location, preferably close to a source of water. Be sure to cover the materials with a tarp when you stop work for the day.

To start a batch of mortar, shovel in the sand first. Then add the other ingredients specific to your mix. Use a mortar hoe to dry-mix the ingredients until you get a uniform color. Pull the dry mix to one end of the mixing pan, and add 1 gallon (3.8 L) of water at the opposite end. Using the hoe, begin pulling sections of the dry mix into the water, mixing the two with a chopping action. Pull the wet mortar to the opposite end of the dry mix, add more water, and repeat the process until all the dry mix is wet. If more water is

necessary, add it in small increments, because it's easy to add too much water and end up with a soupy mix. There's no set formula for just how much water to add to a particular batch. The dampness of the sand, the desired composition, the absorption rate of the materials, and the weather conditions all have to be taken into consideration. I suggest setting aside a couple of gallons of the dry mix from your first batch just in case a batch becomes too wet.

Continue mixing the mortar with a chopping action to thoroughly mix in the water. Pockets of the dry mix tend to accumulate in the corners and on the very bottom of the mixing pan. Check these areas with the hoe. You may have to repeat the process of chopping and pulling the mortar two or three times to completely mix a batch.

MORTAR CONSISTENCY

The mortar used in the dry-stack look is mixed drier than other mortars. It should be slightly sticky, yet still crumbly. Take a handful and pat it into a ball. It should hold together easily. Drop it a couple of feet from one hand to the other. The ball should crumble and fall apart on impact. If you're working in dry, hot weather, the mortar should be mixed slightly wetter, but it should not be soupy.

Set the mortar mixer up on blocks to allow the mortar to dump directly into the wheelbarrow.

When stacking stone with a visible mortar joint or laying mortared paving, the mortar should be as wet as possible without being runny. Mortar of this consistency can be spread easily with a trowel. Consistency of ingredients from one batch to the next is important.

GAS AND ELECTRIC MORTAR MIXERS

Mortar mixers will save time and physical labor, and I recommend one for larger jobs. A small, 4-cubic-foot (.12 m³) mixer will do if you're working alone. If two or more masons are laying stone, a 6-cubic-foot (.18 m³) mixer is needed. Be aware that a mortar mixer is used only to mix mortar and not concrete.

Mortar mixers can be rented on a daily, weekly, or monthly basis. You'll need a vehicle set up for towing in order to haul the mixer to the job site. If you're not familiar with running a mortar mixer, someone at the rental business will explain how to operate it.

WORKING WITH MORTAR

There are three stages of the mortar's curing process. Work you have just completed is *new* or *fresh*. The next day, it's at the *green stage*. When the work is stable, the final stage is *cured*, which happens four to six days later.

If you're working on a 10-foot (3 m) stone wall, you'll be able to lay only several courses before having to take a break. When stonework is in the fresh stage, it's subject to movement, because the mortar hasn't bonded with the stones or set up enough to handle much weight. Rushing the work at this point can cause the stonework to bow outward. Once it's in the green stage, the stonework is a lot more stable, and it won't have any movement at all. Finally, after several days, the mortar will be cured.

VENEER

VENEERED STONE FACING IS A FACADE used to mask concrete or frame-structured walls. The majority of stonework in new home construction is veneered rather than cost-prohibitive solid stone. With a few tools, some mortar, and stone, you'll be able to veneer the exterior of a foundation wall, a concrete block fence, or even an interior wall.

There are different styles of mortared stonework, each influenced by the type, size, and shape of stone used, as well as by how tightly the stones are fit together and by the pattern used. The two main styles are dry-stacked, which is a mortared wall that looks like a dry-stacked wall, and the visible-joint style. Instructions for both styles are included in this section.

Veneering is especially trouble free if the completed project is less than 5 feet (1.5 m) tall. Any taller than that, and you'll need to start using scaffolding or at least a walk board on top of concrete blocks. Also, before beginning, make sure the wall you're about to veneer is fairly plumb.

The recessed mortar in this wall turns the joints into shadow lines, putting more emphasis on the stone's shapes and textures.

Dry-Stack-Look Veneer

This type of stonework has the look of a true dry-stacked stone wall, and you'll use similar building techniques for setting the stones. With the dry-stack look, stones are set using a stiff mortar that's placed between the wall you're veneering and around the back of the stones. With a 6- to 8-inch-thick (15.2 and 20.3 cm) veneer, there's enough depth to stack each course of stone for a dry fit before setting them in mortar. This style of stonework is great for facing concrete foundation walls, block retaining walls, freestanding walls, and interior walls for sunrooms and greenhouse additions (stone provides extra thermal mass).

CONSIDERATIONS

As discussed on page 97, footings evenly distribute the weight of the stonework and safeguard against settling and frost heave. The required thickness for a concrete footing is 8 inches (20.3 cm). If you have a trench that's 2 to 3 feet (.6 to .9 m) deep (because of your frost line), that leaves a lot of space to fill in order to start your stone wall. One option is to lay courses of block on top of the concrete until you've reached the top of the trench. Another option is to fill the entire trench with concrete, which is not that much more expensive.

After the block- or wood-constructed wall is built, you'll need a minimum surface area of 8 inches (20.3 cm) left on the footing to set the stonework.

A mortared stone veneer requires a good selection of workable stone and some patience. This wall sits on top of a sunroom's concrete pad, and concrete block steps are veneered with the same stone.

Wall Ties

With a mortared stone veneer, metal wall ties are used as extra assurance to secure the stonework to the wall being veneered. Wall ties are thin, galvanized metal strips, 7 inches (17.8 cm) long and roughly 1 inch (2.5 cm) wide. With a concrete block wall, the wall ties should be set in the mortar joints when the block wall is laid or with concrete screws if they're set after the block wall has been built. There are two holes in wall ties  for attaching them to the necessary length using one nail or screw. With a wood-frame wall, use one nail (8 penny) to attach each tie to the wood sheathing, preferably in line with the wall studs. Place wall ties roughly every 16 inches (40.6 cm), horizontally and vertically.

The wall ties should be attached to the wall before you begin stacking your veneer.

Optional Materials

Stucco lath is a panel of metal mesh with a honeycomb pattern. It comes in 2½ x 8-foot (.75 x 2.4 m) sheets and can be used in addition to wall ties over a wood-constructed wall. They're hung by setting 1-inch (2.5 cm) nails around the perimeter and down the center. Another option for exterior wood-constructed walls that will be veneered is to use roofing felt as a vapor barrier to cover the sheathing.

This mortared stone veneer covers a wood-sheathed wall with a layer of roofing felt, metal stucco lath, and wall ties.

SELECTING STONE

For tight-fitting stonework, shape your stone as needed. With stones laid along their bedding plane, two flat surfaces are best with at least one good face to show in the wall. Stones stood on their narrow edge may need to be trimmed to produce a surface even enough so it can stand on the course below it. Do all of your trimming off the wall.

If you're not satisfied with the color of a particular stone, it's fine to combine two or more types of stone with different colors. If you do this though, you'll need to mix them evenly to achieve a pleasing blend of color.

HOW MUCH STONE YOU'LL NEED

See page 56 for details.

SITE SETUP

In order to keep the stonework plumb, you'll set the face of each stone 8 inches (20.3 cm) from the wall you're veneering. Choosing a depth (wall thickness) of at least 8 inches (20.3 cm) will give you plenty of options of stone from which to choose. Measure and mark from the face of the block wall to the face of each stone you're setting with a gauge stick or a measuring tape. This will also produce a veneer with an even surface.

PREPARING THE FOUNDATION

In order to lay the dry-stack look for a foundation wall, you'll need a minimum of 6 inches (15.2 cm) of exposed footing to set the stone on, and 8 inches (20.3 cm) is preferable with an 8-inch-thick (20.3 cm) veneer. I've found it common practice in new home construction for only 4 inches (10.2 cm) to be left on the concrete footing after the block foundation is laid. If you want an 8-inch (20.3 cm) veneer, you'll need to express this point to the builder and architect before the home's foundation is laid.

DRY-FITTING THE STONES

After you've prepared your site and attached wall ties and/or stucco laths, you can begin dry-fitting your first course. Dry-fitting the stones with each course allows you to concentrate on getting them to fit just the way you want before they're set in mortar. Read the section on building a dry-laid stone retaining wall on pages 60 through 62 for more information.

Set your cornerstones and wall ends first, and then fill-in between, the way you would with a dry-stone wall. If you're working on a wall more than 20 feet (6 m) long, you may want to dry-fit 10 feet (3 m) of a course at a time and then set that part of the course in mortar. This will allow the first 10 feet (3 m) to begin setting up while you dry-fit the rest of the course. One important consideration is to make sure the wall ties you've secured to the wall line up with the courses as you lay them. You'll be bending the ties into the joints as you add your mortar.

Dry-set stones should have a gravity fit. This means they should stay where you've placed them until you're ready to mortar them into place. This may involve shimming a stone from behind or placing a small, temporary wedge underneath the front edge to hold some stones in place. Combining small, medium, and large stones from one course to the next will make a more pleasing composition.

When laying the stones, avoid placing them with their upper surfaces pitched out toward the wall's face. Stones set this way may slip out of the wall someday. The mortar set at the back of the stonework can be used in the final adjustment of a stone's angle.

Figure 1: Wall ties are worked in between the courses of stonework.

WEEP HOLES

When veneering a concrete block retaining wall, you'll need to add weep holes that allow water that will accumulate behind the wall to pass through it. As the concrete block wall is being built, place 16-inch (40.6 cm) lengths of 2-inch-diameter (5.1 cm) plastic pipe every 4 feet (1.2 m) between the first course of concrete block. Set the pipes 4 inches (10.2 cm) above the foundation's height, extending from the back edge of the block out to where it will be worked into the stone veneer.

CORNERS AND WALL ENDS

Cornerstones will have two faces that meet at a 90° angle. Stones with approximate 90° corners can be alternated with true 90° cornerstones. Set your cornerstones at the wall ends first from one course to the next and then set the stones between them. Taller cornerstones may serve for more than one course of stonework before another is set.

SHINERS

Stones stood on their narrow edge and revealing a large face in the stonework are called *shiners*. Shiners can be as thin as 3 inches (7.6 cm) or as thick as the depth of the veneer (6 to 8 inches [15.2 to 20.3 cm]). Shiners mixed into your veneer break up the pattern and play off the smaller faces to create an interesting look. They're also a great way to take up space. Special attention needs to be paid to these stones while setting them and in building up the stonework around them.

MORTARING THE STONES

If you're veneering a concrete block wall, spray the section you're about to veneer with a hose until it's thoroughly soaked. This will prevent the concrete from sucking moisture out of the mortar. After dry-fitting a portion of the first course, you're ready to set the stones in mortar. Remove several of the stones you've just dry-fit (remembering their order) and spread a 1-inch-thick by 6-inch-wide (2.5 by 15.2 cm) band of mortar at the base of the wall. Set the first cornerstone and proceed with setting the rest of the course.

MORTAR RECIPE

(follow the mixing instructions on page 102).
The mortar recipe for this type of stonework is:
1 part portland cement (type 1)
1 part type 'S' masonry cement
6 parts sand
Water

SECURING THE STONES

To secure a stone in the mortar, push it down or lightly tap it with a hammer. Fill in around the back of the stones with mortar, mixing in rock chips in the larger voids. The backfill should be filled flush with the back edge of each stone's upper surface. Pack the mortar into place around the stones using the end of your trowel's handle or a stick of wood about the same diameter. You can also use your hand to pack the mortar. I usually wear a rubber glove on one hand to do this. The lime in mortar is caustic, and prolonged exposure will pull out the natural oils in your skin. Rinse your hands often and use moisturizing lotion at the end of the day.

To keep from constantly having to reach into the wheelbarrow or mortar pan, place one or two shovels of mortar on top of the veneer already set, slightly ahead of the stones you're about to set. A bucket of mortar by your side is also handy. At the end of each working session, leave the mortared backfill well below the top of the last stones you've worked on.

Located in Linville, North Carolina, this fieldstone veneer is backed up by a concrete block retaining wall that sits on a 2-foot-deep (61 cm) concrete foundation.

When work resumes, you'll fill the space you left during the previous work session with mortar and then continue backfilling. This allows the two mortar sessions to bond better.

As you're working with the mortar, keep it set back from the face of the stonework. Use the drier mortar I've described to work in areas directly behind each stone. I usually have a separate batch of slightly wetter mortar that's easier to work in between the stone's back edges and the block wall. If mortar works its way to the front of the stonework and fills in the joints, leave it to be raked out later.

RAKING THE JOINTS

Once the mortar has set for three hours or so, but hasn't completely hardened, rake back any visible mor-

tar in the joints at least 1 inch (2.5 cm) with a narrow trowel or a stick. Under normal conditions, after four hours, the mortar will have hardened enough to make it difficult to rake it out. If you rake the joints back too soon, you'll notice the mortar will tend to smear. If this happens, wait awhile. Raking the joints is something you have to keep up with throughout a working session. After raking the joints, use a stiff-bristled brush to knock any mortar off the stonework's face.

HARDENED AND CURED MORTAR

The mortar needs to cure slowly to fully bond with the stone. In extremely, hot, dry, windy weather, the mortar set in a wall can dry too fast, causing it to weaken considerably. To keep the mortared stonework from drying too quickly, spray the stonework with a fine mist when the mortar is hard enough not to run or wash out. Then cover the areas you're not working on with plastic sheeting or tarps. At the end of the day, mist the wall again and cover your work. Keep the work dampened and covered for at least a couple of days.

True cornerstones frame this impressive veneer.

THE NEXT COURSES

Continue mortaring all the stones you have dry-fitted until a course is finished. Insert stone chips in the joint below to temporarily support a stone if it feels as if it'll lean out. If you're working with a fairly stiff mortar, you should be able to start your next course immediately. Dry-fit your next course of stone. If you have a number of small faces that create a series of joints close together, select a stretcher stone with a long face to fit over them. When a stone is mortared into place, it should feel secure and not move or rock in any direction.

ADDING SHINERS

To provide a secure surface on which to lay a shiner, you'll need to let the stonework's mortar set several hours. The bottom edge of a shiner should have good

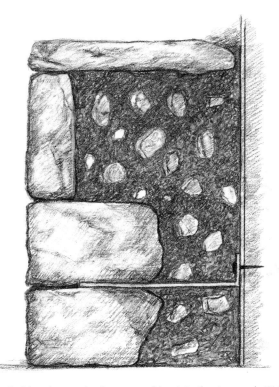

Figure 2: A bond stone ties the narrow shiner into the stonework. Wall ties help secure the veneer to the wall.

contact with the top edges of the stones on which it's sitting. Stand the stone up plumb so its face is in line with the face of the veneer. To keep from constantly having to hold the stone in place, wedge a piece of scrap lumber between its top edge and the block wall. I usually set large shiners back from the wall's face $\frac{1}{2}$ inch (1.3 cm). This provides better contact with the stones that will surround it.

With the stone stood in place, you'll have a large void behind the stone to fill. Carefully work in some mortar behind the stone at its base. Then set the stones to either side of the shiner and continue to backfill behind it using small stones and rock chips mixed in with the mortar. Continue setting the courses of stone, making sure that the stones in contact with the shiner have a tight fit with its edges. When the rest of the stonework is even with the top of the shiner, remove the scrap piece of lumber and set a bond stone across the top of the shiner to tie the stonework back into the full depth of the veneer.

Bond stones span well into the depth or thickness of a wall and add strength to the wall by binding the stonework together. Use a bond stone directly above any narrow stone that only reaches back 3 to 4 inches (7.6 to 10.2 cm) into the veneer.

THE FINAL COURSE

The final course of stone that meets up underneath capstones, the ceiling of an interior wall, or the siding on an exterior wall is a focal point. These stones should be shaped to fit the space they'll fill. Maintain the overall look of the stonework and avoid filling in this last space with a series of smaller stones.

Mortared Veneer Stonework with Visible Joints

Stonework with a visible joint will allow you to use stones that are rougher and more irregular in shape. A mortar joint ½ to ¾ inch (1.3 to 1.9 cm) is a good standard to work with, though 1-inch (2.5 cm) joints (or larger) are fine as long as you're as consistent as possible with the joint size throughout the wall. You'll follow the instructions for the dry-stack look veneer, with these exceptions:

• When you dry-fit the stones as described in the dry-stack look section, leave a ½-inch (1.3 cm) vertical gap between the stones in each course for the mortar.

• The mortar between each course should be set back about 1 inch (2.5 cm) from the stone's face and extend all the way back to the wall you're veneering. Setting the mortar back 1 inch (2.5 cm) will allow for some relief around the individual stones. Each stone should have a uniform mortar joint all the way around it.

• Since the exposed mortar joints are such a visual part of the wall, special attention needs to be given to them. Before the mortar has hardened, you'll need to strike the joints using a slicker trowel. Striking the joints gives them a uniform look and removes any gaps where the mortar meets the edges of the stones. If there are pockets or gaps in the joints, they'll need to be filled with mortar. Use the smaller pointing trowel or a narrow slicker trowel to pack the mortar into place. If the mortar extends out to the face of a stone or beyond, leave it until the mortar has set awhile and lost its watery sheen, then rake it back with a narrow, slicker trowel.

This veneer with visible mortared joints uses a generous number of shiners.

This veneer covers a wood-sheathed wall with a layer of roofing felt, metal stucco lath, and wall ties. A string line is used to set the corner stones. The exposed mortar joints have been raked back dramatically and will be finished later by the mason's helper.

Veneering Inside the Home

Veneering an interior wall involves essentially the same processes as veneering an outside wall, but you need to make sure you have adequate support under the veneer, which means a concrete footing or pad. A proper footing or pad needs to be considered in the designing phase of your home's construction. Consult with a general contractor if veneering an interior wall is an afterthought to your home's original design.

A stone hearth and fireplace surround are the focal point of this living room.

FREESTANDING WALLS

THERE ARE TWO WAYS TO BUILD A FREESTANDING, mortared stone wall. The first one is veneering both sides of a concrete block wall. The other is building a double-faced, solid stone wall. Both methods involve digging and pouring a footer for the walls to sit on.

The capstones on this low, freestanding mortared stone wall were pitched with a hammer and chisel and set to overhang slightly.

Veneered Freestanding Wall

So why bother laying a block wall if you can build a solid stone wall in a similar way? The sole purpose of the block wall is to make it easier to lay the stone, and keep the wall plumb and even in thickness, using the blocks as a gauge. The block wall is a plumb, rigid surface from which to measure, so you end up with an even stone face on each side of the wall. To build a veneered freestanding wall, refer to the veneering instructions on pages 104 through 111 as well as the instructions for laying capstones on page 51.

Both the dry-stack look and the visible mortar joint style will work for this project. You'll need a block wall laid with 4-, 6-, or 8-inch-wide (10.2, 15.2, or 20.3 cm) concrete blocks. These blocks are 8 inches (20.3 cm) tall and 16 inches (40.6 cm) in length. (Concrete blocks are actually $7^5/_8$ inches [19.4 cm] tall, which accounts for a $3/_8$-inch [1 cm] mortar joint that's already figured into the overall measurement.) You'll have a 6- to 8-inch (15.2 to 20.3 cm) veneer on both sides of the block work, which means the stonework will make up 12 to 16 inches (30.5 to 40.6 cm) of the wall's overall thickness (figure 3). Consider how much thicker you want the wall to be and choose one of the three sizes of block listed above. Consult a blockmason or stonemason to help construct the initial block wall.

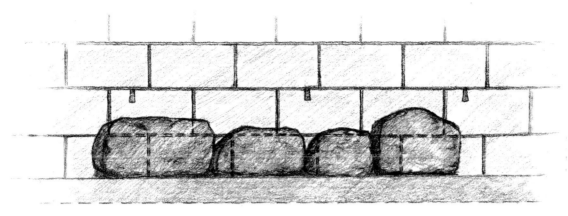

Figure 3: Beginning construction of a veneered freestanding wall

FOOTER WIDTH

The width of your concrete footing should be 12 inches (30.5 cm) wider than the thickness of the wall, for walls up to 4 feet (1.2 m) tall. For walls taller than that, the foundation should be twice the width of the wall's thickness.

DESIGN CONSIDERATIONS

If this is a low wall, 2 to 3 feet (.6 to .9 m) tall, use the thinner, less imposing 4-inch (10.2 cm) blocks. On the other hand, if this is a perimeter wall that's in a large, open space, you may want to use the 8-inch (20.3 cm) blocks, which will make the wall thicker, giving it a more substantial look. For either the dry-stack look or the visible mortar joint style, follow the instructions described earlier in this section for laying the stone.

MORTAR RECIPE

(Follow the mixing instructions on page 102.)

The mortar recipe for this type of stone work is:

2 parts portland cement (type 1)

1 part type 'S' masonry cement

3 parts sand

Water

OTHER CONSIDERATIONS

• Remember to place wall ties in the block work every 16 inches (40.6 cm), both vertically and horizontally, as the concrete blocks are laid.

• The height of the block wall you're veneering is critical to the overall finished wall height. For this reason, you'll need to figure the number of courses of blocks necessary for the wall's height, while allowing room for the thickness of your capstones. For example, if you want the wall's finished height to be 3 feet (.9 m), you'll need 4 courses of concrete blocks, which equals 32 inches (81.3 cm). That will leave you enough space to set capstones.

Freestanding Solid-Stone Wall

Low freestanding stone walls 3 feet (.9 m) high are a beautiful way to separate your front yard from the neighborhood sidewalk or to border a patio. A taller freestanding wall, 4 to 5 feet (1.2 to 1.5 m) tall, is a substantial barrier, providing privacy and, if positioned properly, protection for plants and humans from harsh winds.

To build a freestanding mortared wall, you'll incorporate many techniques that appear in other sections

of this book. You'll follow the instructions for the free-standing dry-laid wall on pages 43 through 52, the instructions on footers and mortar that appear earlier in this section (pages 98 through 103), as well as the veneering instructions on pages 104 through 111.

Along with these instructions, remember the following:

• For best results, mortar one layer at a time. In other words, you'll lay one course, and then lay the course on the opposite side before moving up to the next course.

• Use the mortar recipe on page 115.

• The middle of each course should be filled with mortar, pieces of rocks, and/or blocks and bricks.

Left: This low, freestanding solid-stone wall was stacked without visible mortar joints. Wide bands of mortar spread across the joints in the top of the wall will keep moisture out.

Below: A solid-stone freestanding bench wall zig zags through the J. C. Raulston Garden in Raleigh, North Carolina.

PAVING

WITH THIS PROJECT YOU'LL LEARN TO WORK with flagstone and mortar to create a beautiful hardscape feature, such as a patio, landing, or walkway. Flagstone (flagging) is a general term used to describe stone used for paving. The crab orchard flagstone used in the project below is a medium to dense sandstone from eastern Tennessee. In this project, the flagstone is used as a veneer or overlay for a concrete pad.

A low, mortared stone retaining wall and mortared flagstone paving create an intimate spot to gather in the evening around a fire ring.

Paving Your Site

You may decide to pave an open area or one that abut's a building's foundation wall. The instructions here will cover both scenarios. Your concrete pad will be the standard 4 inches (10.2 cm) thick, with a 1-inch (2.5 cm) bed of mortar and 1-inch-thick (2.5 cm) flagstone. This means the area you'll dig will be 6 inches (15.2 cm) deep. As with dry-laid paving, make sure the flagstone surface is at least 6 inches (15.2 cm) below any building siding.

CONSIDERATIONS

The simplest way to lay a flagstone surface is in a random pattern, with mortar joints averaging 1 inch (2.5 cm) in width. With this random pattern, you'll design as you go by simply setting the pieces in a manner that's pleasing to your eye, keeping in mind to mix the small, medium, and larger pieces, along with any odd colors, for an even and balanced-looking pattern. For a more controlled mortar-joint width and custom design, you'll need to cut and break away sections of most of the pieces of flagging, which takes time and effort.

SELECTING STONE

For a random placement design, use broken pieces of flagging instead of those with cut edges. Cut flagstone will work for this project but is considerably more expensive. Cut stone refers to flagging that's sawn into dimensional pieces, such as rectangles. Random pieces of flagging are sold by weight, while cut stone is priced by the square foot.

Pieces from ¾ to 3 inches (1.9 to 7.6 cm) thick work best. The flagstone you choose should have an even but gritty surface that offers good traction. A

Blue slate is a beautiful and durable paving material.

medium-density stone will hold up well under normal use around the home, while denser stone may be necessary if the project is in a public area where there's a considerable amount of foot traffic.

DELIVERING FLAGSTONE

If you're lucky, the stone yard's delivery truck will have a boom on it that can mechanically remove the pallets at your site. Otherwise, the stone will have to be dumped or off unloaded manually. If you plan on unloading the pieces by hand, you'll need to discuss this with stone yard because of the extra time involved. Dumping thin flagstone on a hard surface can compromise its quality considerably. To absorb some of the shock to the stone in these situations, spread a layer of bark mulch at least 8 inches (20.3 cm) thick or stack several empty pallets exactly where the stone will land. Separate your stone into piles of large, medium, and small pieces. If the flagstones have soil caked on them, hose them off as you separate them.

HOW MUCH STONE YOU'LL NEED

If you're using a thin flagstone, 1 to 1½ inches (2.5 to 3.8 cm) thick, you'll get an average of 150 square feet (13.5 m²) per ton (.9 t) of stone. With 3-inch-thick (7.6 cm) flagging, you'll be able to cover an area of approximately 75 square feet (6.8 m²).

SITE SETUP

Maybe you already have a concrete patio and you're tired of looking at its plain surface. Even if the concrete is old and slightly deteriorated, it may still be usable, and a stone patio will protect the concrete from further decay. For the concrete pad to be suitable, it should be intact, with no large open cracks or sections that have actually separated from the larger mass. Small cracks and areas where concrete has chipped away from the surface are acceptable. They'll get filled in with mortar as you set the flagstone.

An old concrete surface will need to be cleaned to ensure that the mortar adheres properly. Scouring the concrete surface with a bleach and water solution and a stiff brush is one way. You can also have the surface pressure-washed. For removing algae buildup, spilled oils, and other contaminants, apply a solution of hydrochloric (muriatic) acid and water mixed in equal parts. Use a stiff fiber brush on a long han-

dle to spread the solution and scrub stubborn areas. Thoroughly rinse the surface with water. When using muriatic acid, follow the directions on the container. Use extreme caution when handling the acid, and wear rubber gloves and eye protection when applying this solution.

Creating Your Own Concrete Pad

Setting mortared flagstone is a doable project for most anyone; setting up for and pouring the concrete pad may be a stretch for some people. If this is the case, you may want to hire a mason or carpenter to do the concrete work for you. Follow the instructions on page 98 and the information on creating a form for pouring the pad yourself.

Random pieces of blue sandstone flagging are set in an eye-catching design. The mortared flagstone surface is durable and relatively maintenance-free.

STAKING OUT THE PAD'S PERIMETER

See page 87. But in this case, make sure to mark the perimeter outside your planned area, since you're pouring a concrete pad, which requires the use of plywood forms. See pages 87 through 89 for information on determining the pitch, removing sod, and grading the site. If you have a concrete pad in place and it's not pitched, you can create a pitch to the stone surface by starting with a thicker base of mortar at one end and decreasing the amount beneath the stones as you move to the opposite end.

BUILDING THE FORM

Once you have graded the site and created the proper pitch, you need to create the form work to hold in the concrete. The upper edge of the form work represents where the top of the concrete pad will be. It's critical to get this edge set correctly to accommodate the thickness of the pad. The form work doesn't have to be beautiful, but it does need to be strong enough to contain the concrete during pouring without bowing or moving. Dimensions for your pad's form work will be specific to your site, as the forms are built into the area you created for the pad.

Begin by using a circular saw to rip 4-inch-tall (10.2 cm) pieces of ³/₈-inch (1 cm) plywood that match the dimensions of your graded area. You'll need only three lengths if your fourth wall is the home's foundation. For this side, you'll need pressure-treated expansion joint material, which you'll place between the poured concrete and the wall. If your design involves curves, hose the plywood down a couple of times; it bends easily when wet. Then pound 12-inch (30.5 cm) 2 x 4 or 2 x 2

Four-inch-wide (10.2 cm) strips of plywood supported by narrow stakes mark the perimeter for the concrete pad that will be poured for a flagstone patio.

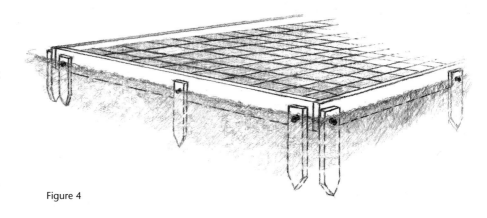

Figure 4

stakes into the ground. Place the stakes along the outside of the plywood every 2 feet (.6 m), with extra at the corners. Drive screws to secure the forms to the stakes (figure 4).

POURING THE CONCRETE

See page 98 for detailed instructions on pouring concrete. You'll suspend heavy-gauge reinforcing wire in the middle of the concrete pad. If the pad receives minor cracks, the wire is there to hold the concrete in place.

Once your concrete pad is in place, allow it to cure for 48 hours before working on top of it. If the weather is hot and dry, keep the pad damp so the concrete will cure slowly. Spray the concrete surface several times during the day for two days from the point it has set up enough so that the water won't wash away the surface of the concrete.

Steel-toothed landscaping rakes can be used to evenly distribute poured concrete.

REMOVING THE FORM WORK

After the concrete has set up for 24 hours, you can remove the form work. Unscrew the stakes and pry the strips away from the concrete.

DRY-FITTING THE FLAGGING

Dry-fitting a section of paving gives you time to get the desired fit between the flagstones before you set them in mortar. At the top of the pitched site, start at a corner or along an outside edge of the pad and work your way across the pad. You want to start along the top edge of the sloped pad so that if it rains you can cover your work and not worry about the rainwater running down the slope into fresh mortar. The same holds true if you need to hose down the pad or stones while working.

Begin with a 4-foot-square (.36 m²) area. Look for angles and curves that complement each other and line them up together. Once you have a few pieces laid out, it's easier to see how other pieces will work in the puzzle. Pieces with long straight edges work well along the outside edges of the concrete pad. Blend the larger pieces with the medium and smaller ones. Look

Pieces of flagstone being dry-fit before they're set in mortar

for pieces that have at least one matching edge to the pieces already laid out. If a portion of one piece overlaps another one you've already laid out, you'll need to mark and break away that portion. Don't forget to leave room for mortar joints. If you're laying a totally random pattern, you won't need to be as critical with the placement of the flagging or the width of the mortar joints.

SETTING THE FLAGGING IN MORTAR

To mortar the pieces in place, you'll have to move them from the dry-fit position in order to spread the mortar (take a mental picture of the layout before

Use stones with long, straight edges to work along the perimeter of square and rectangular concrete pads.

moving the pieces). When you're first starting out, you may want to use a crayon or piece of chalk to mark along the outside edge of the pieces you have dry-fit. This will give you a reference point for spreading the mortar. Work with four to six pieces at a time. See page 101 for instructions on mixing mortar.

Using a shovel, place a couple scoops of mortar onto the pad where you have just removed the dry-fit flagstone. Spread the mortar out with a trowel to a minimum thickness of 1 inch (2.5 cm). Thinner flaggings will need more mortar, while the thicker pieces will require less.

Select an outside edge or corner piece from the dry-fit section and lay it down on top of the bed of mortar, pressing it into the mortar, and you're on your way. If the mortar is the correct consistency, you'll be able to push the stone into the mortar. If it's a bit stiff, you may need a rubber mallet to encourage it into place.

Use a level to check the angle of each stone as it's set.

CHECKING FOR PITCH AND LEVEL

Use the 4-foot (1.2 m) level to check the pitch of the piece's surface with the necessary slope, then turn the level 90° to check for level. Depending on how even the surface of a piece is, you may have to move the level around, taking several readings for a particular area and working with an average reading. After setting a few sections of dry-fit stones, you'll be able to set the pieces by eye and then double check by using the level. With the first section of flagging set in mortar, you'll be ready to go on and dry-fit another section.

OTHER CONSIDERATIONS

• As you work the flagging into place, you'll notice that along the outside edge of the section you're setting there will be small amounts of extra mortar left from when you pushed a piece of flagstone into place. Keep this mortar cut back flush with the outside edges of the pieces you have just laid. Use your trowel to cut the mortar back to be reused. Make sure the mortar is cut back along this edge at the end of a working session so you have a clean edge to work up to when you return.

• If you're working in shade or partial shade, the mortar, the pad's surface, and the stones will be cooler, allowing for plenty of working time. If a batch of mor-

Once a piece is set, cut away the excess mortar around its edges. Be sure that the mortar is flush with the edges of the stone at the end of each working session so you'll have a clean edge when you resume work on the project.

tar is wetter than necessary, let it set for five to ten minutes before setting the flagging. You can then work on dry-fitting another section. When working in direct sun on a hot, dry day, the mortar sets up much more quickly. One way to slow things down is to occasionally use a hose to mist the stones and the pad. A damp concrete pad and damp stones are fine; though you don't want the concrete pad soaking wet with standing water when you're ready to spread mortar.

• Once a batch of mortar is mixed, it needs to be used within about one hour, depending on how wet the mortar is. To keep the mortar from drying out too quickly, keep it consolidated in a mass in the wheelbarrow or mortar pan and cover it with a folded tarp or scrap of plywood.

GROUTING THE MORTAR JOINTS

There are a couple of ways to grout your mortar joints. One is to do the grouting as you go along, which makes a better bonding of mortar between the joints and the concrete pad. On larger projects, this is best accomplished by having one person set the flagging and another grout the joints. If you're working alone, grouting slows the process of getting the pieces set in place, as it can get a bit tedious. You can save grouting until the end of the project and get the satisfaction of laying the stones out first. If you do this, be sure to leave the joints fairly clean of mortar, while leaving the mortar at the bottom of each joint alone.

Though it's not hard or heavy work, grouting does take some concentration while you're in a sitting or kneeling position. Kneepads or garden pads made of dense foam are a must when grouting.

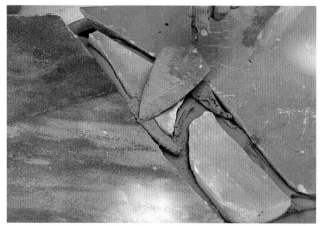

Use a pointing trowel to cut away sections of mortar about the thickness of the joint you're filling. Work the mortar into the joint. It should be flush with the surfaces of the flagstones.

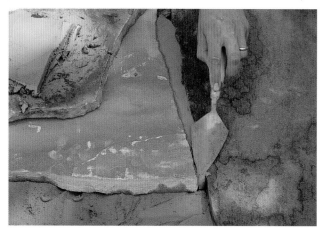

Press down firmly with the trowel to completely fill the joint with mortar.

GROUTING TECHNIQUES

Work the mortar between the joints with a pointing trowel or a small duckbill trowel. A small section of plywood, a short section of scrap 2 x 10 lumber, or one of the pavers works well to spread on the mortar for grouting. Place approximately 1 quart (.95 L) of mortar on your board and spread it out evenly about 1 inch (2.5 cm) thick in a more or less rectangular shape.

With your trowel, cut away a narrow strip of mortar about the width of the mortar joint you're working on. The mortar should be stiff enough to hold this shape. Work the mortar into the joint, pushing it down along

the length of the joint. Add more until the mortar is even with the surface of the stones. Take your time and keep the amount of smeared mortar on the surface of the stones to a minimum. Immediately wipe away any mortar that does smear with a sponge or wet rag. Work the mortar with your trowel until the surface of the mortar is even and fairly smooth.

When you're setting the first couple sections of flagstone, the mortar joints will be filled while working on top of the concrete pad. The mortared flagging will need to set up for one hour on a warm and dry day, and more if it is a cold and damp day, before you can put your weight on them. Carefully step or kneel on the center of the larger flagstones to avoid putting pressure on their edges and the smaller pieces until they have cured for half a day.

BRUSHED AND SMOOTH MORTAR JOINTS

There are a couple of ways to treat the surface of the grouted mortar. One is to leave it smooth after you trowel the joint. A smooth mortar joint tends to show the trowel marks easily, and you may actually like that look. Another option is to lightly brush the grout surface with a flexible bristle brush. To do this, allow the

Finish the joint's upper surface by leaving it troweled and smooth, or wait for the mortar to lose its watery sheen and then brush its surface with a masonry brush for a grainy finish.

smooth mortar to set up until it loses its glossy sheen. Then lightly brush over the mortar until it has a coarse look to it. A coarse finish hides trowel marks left in the joint and looks a little more subdued than the smooth sheen. Both finishes are fine; it really depends on your preference. Try a little of each at the beginning of the project, and then, for the sake of a consistent look, stick with one.

FINAL THOUGHTS

• Keep your work area swept clean, particularly areas of the pad where you're about to spread mortar and set flagstones.

• Cover newly finished paving if the weather is extremely hot, dry, and windy, or if it's about to rain. Covering the work will slow the setting-up time and the mortar's curing process, which reduces cracks in the mortar and improves the bonding of mortar and stone.

• Allow the mortar to cure for several days before you put any furniture on a newly paved surface.

Creating a Fire Ring

Fire rings are used to keep a fire contained in a designated area. A successful fire ring on a patio needs a hole in the concrete pad that allows rainwater to filter through. Without the hole, rainwater would fill the ring and cause ashes and charred wood to float out and across the patio.

Decide where you want your ring and create the necessary form work around the area you planned for the ring. When you're designing a fire ring, special consideration needs to be given to the size of the fires

you'd like to have. The interior diameter of the fire ring pictured here is roughly 30 inches (76.2 cm). Any ring smaller than 24 inches (61 cm) in diameter will permit only relatively small wood to be used.

Pour the concrete for the pad, and remove the form work used to create the ring 48 hours later. Dig an 18-inch (45.7 cm) hole in the circle using a posthole digger and a shovel. Fill the hole with 8 to 10 inches (20.3 to 25.4 cm) (depending on how deep you want your "pit" to be) of 1-inch (2.5 cm) gravel.

Use metamorphic or igneous stone for your ring, and make sure the rocks are similar in height and shape with edges that match up well. Avoid extremely

Set the tallest stone first and use different amounts of mortar to fit the rest of the stones to the same height as the first stone.

First the stones are dry-laid, and then a pointing trowel is used to work the mortar around the stones.

soft stones that will crumble when exposed to extreme heat. Keep the height of the stones between 8 to 10 inches (20.3 to 25.4 cm), making it easier to work on the fire while allowing more light to spill out from the ring.

Dry-fit the stones first. Place them on the edge of the concrete pad and use wedges to keep the stones from falling over. Once you're satisfied with the look of the ring, mix your mortar (use the recipe on page 115) and begin mortaring your ring in place. Remove your tallest stone first and place a 2-inch (5.1 cm) base of mortar on the exposed section of pad. Push the stone into the mortar and carefully pack the mortar around the base of the stone on the inside and outside of the ring. Work the mortar around the base of the stone up to 2 inches (5.1 cm). Set the remaining stones using a level to adjust their height and extra mortar to make them level to the tallest stone. After the stones are mortared into place, set the flagstone for the patio right up to the outside of the ring (masking the exposed mortar).

Paving an Interior Hearth

The hearth pictured below is one that I built for my friends Jackie and Evan in their new home. Evan built the house and worked with me on this project. The hearth took us about half a day to complete. Its design can be adapted to fit most any situation involving a freestanding wood stove or a vented gas-burning unit. The stone for the hearth is a locally quarried, metamorphosed granite and shist rock with obvious bands of quartz and speckled mica throughout its structure. The wood-burning stove sitting on the completed hearth has a soapstone exterior.

CEMENT BOARD

Interior cement board is a rigid material made of a aggregated portland cement core with a fiberglass mesh coating. It's typically used in house construction as a masonry surface for applying ceramic tile. It comes in 3 x 4 or 3 x 5-foot (.9 x 1.2 or .9 x 1.5 m) sheets with a $5/16$- or $1/2$-inch (8 mm or 1.3 cm) thickness and is available at most building supply and home improvement stores.

The cement board is set on top of a $3/4$-inch (1.9 cm) plywood subfloor, nailed to a doubled-up 2 x 8 floor joist. Evan doubled up the floor joist directly

This simple stone hearth can be altered to fit almost any interior setting.

beneath the hearth area to handle the extra weight of the stone and a 400-pound (182 kg) stove. If you're setting a hearth on a wood-framed floor, consult with a carpenter or building contractor for a professional opinion of how to deal with the extra weight in your particular situation.

SETTING THE CEMENT BOARD

Mark the measurements of your hearth's design on the subfloor using a tape measure and a chalk box to strike the lines, or a pencil and a 4-foot (1.2 m) level as a straight edge to make your marks, then cut the cement board to fit in this area. You can score the cement board with a utility knife and break it along the scored

line. Or use a jigsaw with a masonry blade, which allows you to cut with more control.

To provide an absolutely even surface for the cement board, spread a ¹⁄₂-inch (1.3 cm) layer of latex-fortified mortar (follow the directions provided on the bag), using a notched tile-setter's trowel. Lay the cement board down and secure it in place with 1¹⁄₂-inch (3.8 cm) roofing tacks or all-purpose screws.

STONE SELECTION

Stones with an even surface provide a more stable area on which to set the wood stove and will be easier to keep clean. Stones with major protrusions and uneven surfaces may require some shimming under the stove's legs to secure them. The stone used for the hearth pictured here averaged 1¹⁄₂ inches (3.8 cm) in thickness. Fieldstone, flagstone, and slate will all work for this project.

DRY-FITTING THE STONES

Start dry-fitting the stones around the perimeter of the cement board, then work toward the center. Trim the stone's edges, when necessary, to create joints that average ³⁄₄-inch (1.9 cm). Check for level before continuing.

Dry fit the hearth stones on top of the secured cement board.

Dry fit smaller pieces of stone in the gaps.

MORTARING THE STONES

To set the stones, mix a batch of mortar described on page 115, and follow the directions for setting flagstone on pages 121 through 123. The mortared joints in this project were completed with a brushed finish (page 124). To complete the project, Evan used a band of red oak trim to frame the hearth and match the oak flooring.

SPECIAL CONSIDERATION

If the wood stove is extremely close to a wall, a fire barrier is required to satisfy fire safety codes. Check with your building inspector for local requirements.

A red oak trim was added after the stones were mortared but before the joints were grouted.

Chapter 5

THE ROMANCE OF STONE

What's so evocative and/or ethereal about placing stones and boulders in a field or garden? What is it about a stone that would make somebody start chiseling pieces out of it to create a sculpture? I can't answer these questions for everyone, but I know that for myself, there are many possible reasons. Perhaps stone is one of the last primal links to our past association with nature. Or maybe it's a way of creating a new narrative for something that may have existed when our prehistoric ancestors were first shaping stone hand axes and arrowheads. I don't know, maybe there's also something in us that wants to leave something behind—a message for future generations. Or it could be none of the above. Decide for yourself.

STONE CARVING

THE SURFACE OF STONE HAS BEEN USED as a medium to record human history since the Stone Age. The caves of Lascaux, France, and the Four Corners region of the U.S. Southwest come to mind, where interior walls and exposed rock faces were painted and carved with pictographs and petroglyphs. Abstract forms and figurative images depict a culture of archaic societies and their ancestral gods. Geometric figures, including circles, squares, triangles, dots, and spiraling images are grouped with stylized renderings of human and animal figures, representing some of the first human art and recorded history.

Early Greek and Roman classical architecture developed building styles using carved stone features that are emulated in today's modern buildings. Ancient stonecutters produced cylinders from large cubes of stone and stacked them to create massive columns. Hand-carved chamfered, or beveled, edges were added to building stones as decorative features and for the practical purpose of directing rain off windowsills, door and window openings, and where courses of stone stepped in. Detailed, decorative stone carving evolved into exquisite classical molding, ornate lettering, gargoyles, and statues.

The name of a building and the date it was begun are often carved onto the flat plane of a building's cor-

The Wheel of Life is a Tibetan symbol carved in stone located along a path on the Tibetan Plateau, Nepal.

This example of two-dimensional relief is part of a large stone carving called *Arjuna's Penance*, located in Maha Bali Puram, India.

nerstone or a date stone in low relief. Gravestones memorialize individuals with inscribed dates of birth and death, poetry and proverbs.

Carving and Creativity

Using a hammer and chisels to carve stone requires focused attention and a certain amount of hand-eye coordination. If you're used to working with your hands, you probably have this sense of dexterity; if not, it's something you'll acquire through practice. I worked on a potter's wheel for five years, which required a similar mind-set in order to bring a lump of clay to center on a spinning wheel-head. Similarly, the act of stone carving brings you into the present moment with the stone, a few simple tools, and your imagination.

With minimal setup time, you can carve just about anywhere. I've carved on stone while vacationing at the beach, in my backyard, and during a camping retreat next to a mountain stream. My small tool bag holds a variety of chisels, filing tools, hammers, sandpaper, and pieces of stone, ready to go just about anywhere.

A two-dimensional high-relief stone carving

Stone on Stone is a simple leaf motif carved from gneiss by Steve Watts. He used a napped hand picker made from a piece of ryolite stone.

Observation and Inspiration

I remember the first time I observed a stone carver working on a piece of sculpture. The sculpture started out as a large cube of marble 3 feet (.9 m) wide and 5 feet (1.5 m) tall, set on a dolly that was wheeled across a large outdoor concrete pad when needed. I could see that the sculpture was going to be abstract from a sketch set on the carver's workbench. He began carving with stout chisels attached to an air hammer that was powered by a large air compressor. The mass of marble started to take shape within a couple of hours. In a fury of motion, large sections of the stone were weakened around the edges and broken off while smaller chips went flying in every direction, accompanied by a cloud of dust. It was quite a dramatic display.

A year ago, I met Tom Jackson, a stone carver living in central Tennessee, who works primarily with Indiana limestone. Tom carves pieces used for architectural purposes. While I was visiting, he was working on a mantel and the supporting pieces that surround a fireplace. His method of carving is very methodical. Each step is carefully thought out, accompanied by a series of drawings and carefully executed carving techniques.

The initial shaping of a piece of limestone with an air hammer and chisel

Tom Jackson marks the remaining area he'll carve to complete a series of ribbons that complement the geometric pattern.

Tom uses a circular saw with a diamond blade to remove large sections of stone. By cutting a series of *curfs* (grooves) into areas of stone to be removed, the stone is weakened enough so that the toothlike pieces can be knocked off with a hammer. The high spots left where the stone breaks away are carved down to an even layer with an air hammer and chisels. As the work gets more detailed, Tom shifts to smaller air hammers and smaller chisels.

Stone Sources

You can find good carving stone through the Internet, though shipping will be expensive. Check with your local university. If it has an art department, chances are it'll have a sculpture studio with some stone around or know about the closest source. Or somebody in the art department may know about local sculpture carvers who can point you in the right direction. At the very least, visiting these spots may present an opportunity to learn something about the carving process. Stone yards will most likely have sandstone (flagstone) in 2- to 3-inch-thick (5.1 to 7.6 cm) slabs that can be carved into two-dimensional designs with low and high relief.

GOOD CARVING STONES

Soapstone is a crystalline-metamorphic stone available in a wide variety of colors and is extremely easy to carve and polish. Alabaster is a dense, translucent stone similar to soapstone that's only slightly harder.

Soft- and medium-density sandstone are good, inexpensive materials to start out with for a low-relief design.

Oolitic limestone, typically found in Indiana, U.S. and Portland, England, is good for two- and three-dimensional carving because it's the younger of the two types of limestone and easier to carve. Calcite limestone is also workable but slightly harder. Limestone chips easily, so be careful when you're carving and handling the stone, particularly if you have a design with a raised relief.

Granite is one of the hardest stones around and is probably best avoided by the novice carver. The crystals in granite have been fused together by great heat and pressure, which make the techniques for shaping granite less like carving and more akin to crushing the stone's surface with large pointing chisels and hammers to get the sculpture's initial shape.

GREEN STONE

It's widely agreed among stonemasons and carvers that freshly quarried stone, also know as green stone, is easier to break and carve

Carved from granite, *Javaman's Demitasse*, by Verena Schwippert is for the serious coffee aficionado.

The east stone of the inner circle at Clyde Hollifield's home honors the mammals indigenous to the Southern Appalachian Mountains and commemorates the sunrise.

than seasoned or hardened stone. Newly quarried stone contains a certain amount of groundwater, referred to as *quarry sap* that will slowly evaporate once the stone is exposed to the atmosphere (with the stone reaching its hardest state in a few years). The difference between green and hardened stone is most critical with harder stone, such as granite, but even limestone will become more brittle and less malleable as it air cures.

Getting Started

You can start carving on stone by investing in a few chisels and a hammer. Craft supply shops should have catalogs to order stone-carving tools. You can also locate tools on the Internet. To familiarize yourself with the hammers and chisels, start by carving on small pieces of stone without worrying about how the carvings will turn out. Try carving on several types of stone, from soft to medium density, to decide which appeals to you the most.

Tools

You'll need a **hammer** (mallet) for carving with chisels. Choose one that's 1 to 2½ pounds (.45 to 1.1 kg).

Bush hammers have toothed surfaces used to round off edges of stone and create a frosted rough surface.

Wooden hammers are used when carving in delicate areas of a design.

A **point chisel** has a single point that's used to etch lines of a design in low relief carving and for knocking off larger chunks of stone when roughing out a three-dimensional shape.

Toothed chisels are used to remove layers of stone.

Chris Berti uses a hammer and point chisel to chip away larger sections of stone

These chisels will leave marks that look like rows of ridges and grooves. Work the chisel across these rows to create a series of smaller high and low spots that can be chiseled down with a flat chisel.

Flat chisels with straight beveled edges are used for shaping and removing layers of stone.

Gouging chisels are used to scoop or dig out the interior surface of a bowl or decorative fluted shapes, such as a series of rounded, parallel grooves. The cutting edges of gouging chisels vary from half round to slightly curved.

A flat chisel is used to carve deeper relief.

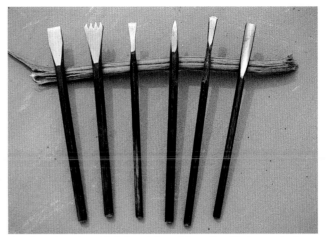

A variety of carving chisels from left to right: a flat chisel, a toothed chisel, a round-edged chisel, a point chisel, a quarter-round gouge chisel, and a half-round gouge chisel

Riffler files have a coarse, metal surface made up of a series of $1/16$-inch (2 mm) and shorter sharp, angled studs. They're used for shaping and smoothing over stone surfaces. Rifflers range in size from 6 to 14 inches (15.2 to 35.6 cm).

Rasps are half-round rough metal files used to clean up scratch marks before sanding a stone's surface.

Riffler files

Bracelet rasps are shaped like a stiff, round bracelet with a rough surface that's perfect for shaping the interior of a concave shape.

Files have a finer surface than rasps and are used to file down the

Chris uses a metal file to further refine the surface.

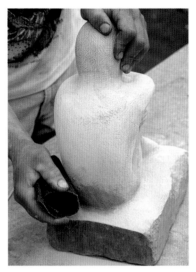

Chris Berti using a coarse, high-resin sanding belt from a belt sander to remove ridges and high spots from his sculpture

marks left by a rasp, taking the stone to a smoother surface.

A **wire brush** is needed to clean the surfaces of rasps and files when they get gummed up with stone dust.

Handsaws have coarse-toothed blades that can be used to shape raw pieces of softer stone, such as soapstone and alabaster.

Hacksaws have fine-toothed blades used for finer work on softer stones. These saw blades fill up with stone dust and need to be cleaned often.

Sandpaper and **sanding cloths** are used to help finish a carved stone's surface. Use 60- to 400-grit sandpaper for a coarse finish and 600- to 800-grit for a final, smooth surface.

Sand bags or a **stone banker** filled with sand offer a malleable surface in which to secure smaller pieces of stone. A bed of sand helps to evenly distribute the shock from impacting hammers and chisels on a stone's surface.

Use **chalk**, a **pencil** or **greaseless crayon** to draw your design on the stone you're about to carve. Avoid using felt-tip markers, as they tend to bleed into stone.

Safety glasses are imperative when carving stone. A flying stone chip can cause a lot of damage to an unprotected eye.

Dust masks are uncomfortable but should be considered. Always work in an open, well-ventilated space.

Two-Dimensional Carving

A design drawn out on paper is easily transferred to a stone's surface with a piece of soapstone. If you're planning to build a stone wall, you may want to carve a date stone to signify the time of the project, or a few paving stones with carved relief can be worked into the paving's design, adding an interesting design element. My friend Clyde Hollifield, carved a low relief of whales, a bear's paw, and simple geometric elements,

This 8-inch-diameter (20.3 cm) labyrinth is carved into the top of a small boulder that stands 2 feet, 6 inches (.75 m) tall, and is located at Kirkridge Conference Center in Bangor, Pennsylvania.

such as circles and triangles, into several of the stones in his stone circle. Recently I visited a garden where stones were carved with the words "peace," "harmony," "faith," and "wellness" and set conspicuously along a garden path.

A flat piece of sandstone or limestone, with a minimum thickness of 6 to 8 inches (15.2 to 20.3 cm), is suitable for a wide range of designs. A simple design could include inscribing letters or numbers in a bas-relief, with the remaining surface left intact. Or you could do the reverse: Carve the stone away from the edges of the design to create a distinct foreground and background.

Jim Morris uses a stick of soapstone to transfer the design for a date stone onto the stone's surface.

The initial inscribing of this low-relief design is nearly complete.

Jim inscribes the lines of his design on the stone's surface. The corner of a worktable is used to wedge and secure the stone in place while carving.

By creating more depth to the background surface, you also open up the opportunity to enhance the design in the foreground. A deeper relief will create stronger shadow lines, bringing the design closer to looking three-dimensional. Texture can be added to the background using toothed chisels, creating a cross-hatch pattern that can be refined with a flat chisel, riffler files, and sandpaper.

Once you have a design drawn onto the stone, you're ready to start carving. Hold the stone in place on top of a sandbag or in a bed of sand on top of a banker (see page 34). Use a point chisel or a pointed edge of a flat chisel at a right angle and tap it with the hammer while moving along the lines of your design. At this point, you're simply creating a shallow line of relief that can then be worked deeper with toothed and flat chisels.

To make the groove slightly wider and deeper, hold a flat chisel at a slight angle, with one edge of the chisel in the groove, and tap it with the hammer, following the groove, carving out another layer. Flat chisels come with narrow and wide blades; use the narrower ones for making curves, such as the rounded sections of a letter. Keep working with the different chisels until you get the depth of relief you desire.

If the stone is soft enough, you can smooth out the grooves by grasping a flat chisel with rounded edges in your hand to work out rough spots. Rifflers can be used at this point for final shaping.

Three-Dimensional Carving

My stone-carving friend Tom Jackson gave me a rectangular piece of limestone to work on while I was photographing him in his studio one day. Being fairly new to carving, I decided to work on a simple, abstract, three-dimensional figure, which I could alter somewhat if I made a mistake while carving. When working with a three-dimensional piece of sculpture, you have to consider the possibility that it may be viewed from any point.

When you're first getting started, keep the design simple while getting used to working with the carving tools and a particular type of stone. In order to reduce the amount of wasted stone, choose a stone that's roughly the size and shape of the finished piece you

A point chisel is used to pitch a line of relief in the limestone.

A simple line of relief is drawn out on a piece of oolitic limestone.

have in mind. Once you've transferred your design onto the stone, follow your lines with the pointed edge of a flat chisel and hammer to produce a narrow, shallow groove that'll be your relief point to work up to. Whenever possible, stay back from your point of relief, working the chisel away from it rather than toward it.

To remove a layer of stone, use a toothed chisel, which leaves rows of ridges and grooves, then work the chisel across the rows to create a crosshatched pattern of high and low spots. Use a flat chisel to remove the high spots, taking the stone down to an even surface. If you want to take the surface down further, repeat the process. Be careful where you point the chisel when working around any area that has a relief carved into it.

CARVING A BOWL

For making a bowl or concave shape in stone, use a gouging chisel or a flat chisel with rounded edges and a hammer. The cutting edge for gouge chisels comes in a variety of curves from slight to half round.

Using a point chisel, start chipping away at the center of the area you've marked for a hollow. Then with a gouge held at a slight angle along the outside edge of the depression you just chipped into the bowl, carve down and toward the center of the hollow. You'll gain

A flat chisel that is slightly rounded off at each end of the cutting edge is used to gouge out a small bowl.

more control of the chisel by grasping it closer to the cutting edge. Circle around the area in the center you've chipped with the point chisel, removing a layer of stone. As you remove stone, the upper edge of the bowl will start to flare, with the center flattening slightly. To go deeper, use the point chisel to chip out the center again and then go back to the gouging chisels.

You may want to leave the interior of the hollow slightly textured, fluted, or completely uniform and smooth. For a smooth, rounded surface, work with a narrow, flat chisel that has rounded edges, removing the ridges and high points. Next, use a bracelet rasp to refine the surface. Finally, use a series of sandpaper (from coarse to fine) for a smooth finish.

SURFACE OPTIONS

Contrasting rough and smooth surfaces can be used as a design element with carved stone. A quick way to leave a gritty, rough surface over larger areas is to use a bush hammer, or for smaller areas and more control, use a frosting tool held like a chisel and struck with a hammer.

For smoother surfaces, work the stone with a flat chisel to remove irregularities left by toothed chisels. Riffler files are used next for final shaping and removing the lines left by a flat chisel. Use silicon carbide screening (100 to 200 grit) or your lowest-grit sandpaper first (100 grit and below) to begin the finishing process. Then move to finer grit sandpaper.

Some of the surface of this carving was left highly textured. For a smoother finish use fine grit sandpaper.

BOULDERSCAPING

BOULDERS CAN BE FOUND in an infinite variety of shapes and sizes and a host of textures and colors. With their mass and weathered surface, boulders have an unassuming nature indifferent to the weather and other activities around them. Boulders, large and small, have many uses in defining a landscape both as an aesthetic and functional element. In an intimate garden setting they engender a sense of tranquillity and elegance; on a windswept knoll, boulders signify permanence.

Small boulders easily add definition to the edge of a paved area, such as a patio or garden pathway. Ledges and rocky outcroppings for alpine gardens are created using a mix of boulders and smaller rocks mixed with gravel. Kids love to climb on large stones set in play areas that, years later, can be transformed into perennial garden beds.

An iron gate hangs between two boulders at the entrance to Columcille, a megalithic park in Bangor, Pennsylvania.

Carefully chosen boulders have a sculptural quality in a landscape, although your reasons for setting boulders may go beyond their aesthetic value to include the desire to create a sacred space. If this is your intention, working with stone is certainly a meaningful way to ground your energy to a particular place.

Some Boulder Wisdom

Large is a relative term when talking about boulders. I refer to a boulder as any stone I can't manually lift. A small boulder could be the size of a laundry basket; a large one could be as big as a bear, or bigger. Technically, a boulder is any stone that has broken free from the bedrock—its parent rock—and sits exposed or buried in soil or rock debris.

Some of my favorite places to view natural boulderscapes are streams and creek beds in the mountains where I live. Many of the streambeds in Western North Carolina are carved out of solid bedrock and strewn with boulders of all shapes and sizes. Here, the natural forces of water and gravity have created some of the most alluring and beautiful settings of stone imaginable. In the warmer months, I scramble up and over the stones barefoot, wading through pools lined with boulders, occasionally siting a brook trout or the rare pitcher plant hanging on a wet, mossy, rock

Following the path of least resistance, water spills through an opening in this natural boulderscape.

ledge. The stream's banks are festooned with boulders and rock outcroppings cultured with rhododendrons, ferns, lichens, and mosses.

If you're considering setting large stones in your landscape, I recommend spending some time observing the natural settings of boulder stones in your local area. Good places to look for natural stone settings are county roads, woodland trails, scenic waterfalls, along abandoned railroad beds, or your local arboretum.

heavy equipment, and in some cases, harvesting these stones will disturb the natural environment. Each year, more native habitat is lost and destroyed, disrupting the delicate ecosystems where many endangered plants and animals make their home. Our impact on these areas is something to be aware of as we strive to naturalize our own backyards.

Weathered and Quarried Boulders

Moss- and lichen-covered boulders with weathered patinas have a more venerable, stately appearance. Newly quarried boulders lack the desirable weathered look, but often you can find unusual and striking shapes, making them suitable candidates for boulderscaping. If you're not satisfied with the raw look of quarried stones and are a person with patience, you may try culturing them. I met a stonemason who cultured his handpicked quarried stones in a mossy ravine. He would dump them in a damp, shady area on his property, and in less than a year's time, they'd be covered with moss, ready to be retrieved.

If you buy boulders from a stone yard or landscape supplier, the weathered stones will be more expensive. This is partly because of the demand, and often they come from remote areas that make gathering them difficult. Gathering boulders requires the use of

A shaggy coat of resurrection ferns, green moss, and Usnea moss enhance the beauty of this stone outcropping.

Locating Boulders

If you live in an area where there's an abundance of stone, you may be lucky enough to locate boulders at bargain rates, possibly free. Most people are clued into the value of stone these days, but, still, there are situations where they can be yours for the cost of moving them from a particular site. My friend and fellow stonemason Joe Roberts and I once built a stone retaining wall using small boulders that were unearthed while a house site was being excavated. The wall is 100 feet (30 m) long, averages 4 feet (1.2 m) in height, and contains approximately 20 tons (18 t) of stone. The owner of the house knew she wanted a retaining

Early morning sunlight creates a dynamic mood for a group of ferns cradled in the cleft of a boulder.

This 2-ton (1.8 t) boulder anchors the end of a dry-stacked retaining wall built by Jeff Nelson.

wall and called me when she saw tons of good usable stone being unearthed during the excavation. Many of the stones that went into the wall were boulders weighing 100 to 400 pounds (45 to 182 kg) and were set using a small ladder. It was because of good fortune and the owner's insight that all the stones we put in the wall came from her extremely rocky property. Some of the larger boulders excavated were used in the berm of the built-up driveway, while others were buried or hauled off by the equipment operator and general contractor.

Smooth, rounded boulders naturally complement water features.

The sculptural qualities of this granite boulder were created at the quarry when it was blasted from a large vein of rock. Over time, natural weathering will enhance the stone's surface. A tuft of moss has made itself a home at the stone's base.

If you live in a more urban or suburban setting, your best bet may be to visit your local stone yards and landscape suppliers. Most of them will have boulders on site or know where to get them.

Design Considerations

When setting a group of boulders, using stones of the same type and color will create a more harmonious and unified placement. Using a variety of shapes and sizes gives a stronger sense of depth and dimension to the overall composition. I look for stones that have interesting characteristics, such as odd angles, rounded features, an interesting texture, or a pleasing color. Avoid soft and flaky stones—ones from which you can easily remove pieces with your hands. These stones won't

These precariously stacked, irregularly shaped stones have taken on an animated, personable quality.

hold up to the weather for long and may not survive being moved.

When you're setting stones in groupings, think about odd numbers of stones such as 3, 5, 7, and 9. It's much easier to create a natural, visually balanced grouping with these numbers in mind. Within each grouping, combine tall, vertical stones with blocky stones half the height of the taller ones, and low, broad stones to visually anchor a grouping.

Point of View

Single boulders and groupings of stones in a landscape may be viewed from a number of angles. The primary view is the most likely angle that the stones will be seen from. This view may be from a pathway leading to your home, a back deck, or a garden bench. Select

the most interesting face of the stones to be viewed from this vantagepoint. The other faces are viewed less often, but are still worth considering while designing.

Consider other features in the landscape that may support or detract from the design. A gentle slope allows a grouping of stones to gain more visual height, which would be necessary if there's a low hedge blocking one of your points of view. A tree trunk may be used as a vertical element to frame one side of a grouping.

Moving Boulders

Small boulders weighing 100 to 300 pounds (45 to 136 kg) can be moved with wheelbarrows, hand trucks, and if the stone has enough flat surface area, with two to three people lifting them. If you have a slope to work with, and the stone needs to go downhill, gravity

Bare trees and long shadows cast by the standing stones mark the waning daylight of a November afternoon at Columcille Megalithic Park.

can be very helpful. Sliding a stone on a wide board is much easier than trying to slide it on the ground. How easily a stone will slide in this situation depends on how smooth the stone is and the degree of the slope. Any stone over 300 pounds (136 kg) will require more manpower, tools, and/or machinery.

TOOLS AND MACHINERY FOR LIFTING BOULDERS

Along with a shovel, mattock, and some pry bars, one or more of these tools or vehicles will help you get your boulders where you want them.

Nylon webbing or straps come in a variety of widths and thicknesses. They don't stretch like rope or leave marks on the stones as chains sometimes do.

You can create loops with **nylon rope** and a webbing strap to hoist a stone.

Various lengths of **chain** come in handy when moving stone. They're easy to work with, durable, and quick to hook up to equipment and stone. The sizes of links in a chain are less important than the alloys in a chain's metal, which determines its strength. Chains with 3/8-inch (1 cm) links are easy to handle and come in three working load limits: 2,500, 5,400, or 6,600 pounds (1,135, 2,452, or 2,996 kg). If you're hoisting stone heavier than 3 tons (2.7 t), consider larger chains or cables.

A **cable** with an eye or loop at each end is great for lifting large boulders and leaves little, if any, scarring on a stone's surface. Cables can be bought through industrial supply houses. Most heavy-equipment operators will have these available, crane operators in particular.

A **tripod** is used in situations where it's impossible to use heavy equipment. Tripod legs should be round, 4 to 6 inches (10.2 to 15.2 cm) in diameter, and at least 12 feet (3.6 m) tall. A tripod used with a come-

Nylon webbing was easily looped around each end of this stone and linked with a length of chain attached to the bucket on a backhoe.

along, block and tackle, or chain pull is a handy setup for moving and adjusting the position of large stones. Walking a stone with the aid of a tripod is done by positioning the tripod legs off center of where the stone sits and in the direction you want the stone to be moved. As you hoist the stone, it's moved to the tripod's new position.

A **come-along** is a small, manually operated device that uses cables or chains hooked to a drum that's driven by a ratchet-type handle. Come-alongs are

A boulder suspended from a chain hoist and tripod

A small tractor slides a boulder up a ramp into a truck bed.

available in different sizes, and they're rated by their pulling power (from 1 to 5 tons [.9 to 4.5 t]). To use a come-along, you need something stationary to secure it to. It can be hooked to a car or truck or a tree with a strap around it. Using a wide board as a runner for the stone to slide on top of reduces the friction, making the work go more smoothly.

Chain pulls have a ratio of gears that allows for less force to be exerted to lift stones of substantial weight, while locking and holding the stone until you're ready to lower it into place. This item is can be attached to the apex of a tripod.

Log rollers 8 to 12 inches (20.3 to 30.5 cm) in diameter can be used to roll a stone across relatively flat ground (see page 27).

A **four-wheel-drive tractor** with a front bucket is good for hoisting stones connected by chain or webbing. Power steering is a big plus when maneuvering substantial weight hanging off the front bucket. A **small loader** or **farm tractor** can handle stones weighing 1,200 to 1,500 pounds (545 to 681 kg). Small loaders can be rented by the day and are easy to operate with a minimum of instruction. With a small tractor or **riding lawn mower,** you can drag a stone close to its designated position and then work it into place with pry bars and rollers. I have, on occasion, backed my truck onto a project site and dropped an 800-pound (363 kg) boulder right into place. In this situation, a liner in the truck bed reduces the stone's friction, making is easier to slide it out of the bed. Bed liners are made of durable, hard plastic molded to fit in truck beds. For this kind of work, I wouldn't be without one.

The narrow, short wheelbase of this small pickup truck is ideal for getting into most locations. The black, hard plastic bedliner makes it easy for two people to slide these small boulders out of the truck bed.

A front loader will increase your efficiency when moving and setting large rocks.

Front loaders are available in a variety of sizes, each with its own lifting capacity—the largest rated at 2 tons (1.8 t). They come with either front forks (like a forklift) or loading buckets. A bucket is more versatile, but harder to see around than the forks. You can also attach a small backhoe arm to this machine for digging and setting small boulders. Front loaders are easy to operate and available at most equipment rental businesses.

A **backhoe** has a hydraulic arm with a digging bucket. Capable of moving in a 180° arc and with a long outward reach, a backhoe is the most versatile piece of equipment for setting boulders up to 3 tons (2.7 t). These are trickier to operate than a front loader and require an experienced operator.

Cranes, track hoes, and boom trucks are needed for moving boulders that weigh more than 3 tons (2.7 t). All of these will require a certified operator and are rented by the hour, including travel time to a site. They generally have their own webbing and cables for moving boulders. If you decide to use stones in this class, I recommend hiring someone familiar with setting boulders, such as a stonemason, landscape designer, or a landscape architect to help you set up. Having your stones on site ahead of time and preplanning where and how they will be placed, will help make the best use of expensive equipment time.

Hooked with a chain to the bucket of a backhoe, a 1-ton (.9 t) stone is carefully worked into place.

A tight configuration of basalt stones demonstrates a bold way to retain a small area along a short slope.

Boulder Placement

In order to achieve a natural and stable appearance when setting the stones, a portion of each stone will need to be buried below ground unless you're using boulders with relatively flat surfaces and bottoms.

To hold a boulder with a flat surface and bottom in place, build up a berm around the stone's base. This will require plenty of soil that compacts well (such as subsoil or road bond). The height of the berm should cover enough of the boulder's base to secure it (figure 1). Some of the boulder's mass will be diminished by the berm, but you won't lose any of its height as it's set on the original grade. Allow the berm to taper (fall away) from the boulder gradually to give its placement a more natural look. Build the berm up in layers of less than 1 foot (30 cm) of soil and pack each one thoroughly with a tamper.

Stones with a relatively flat, wide bottom can be set in a small hole with soil mounded

Figure 1

around its base. Stones with a less stable bottom can be mounded around as well, but will require more compacted soil in a wider mound. Where frost heaving is a consideration, place a layer of 6-mil plastic 6 inches (15.2 cm) below the surface of the mound. This encourages water to run down its slope rather than saturating the mound. A continuous 3-inch (7.6 cm) layer of compacted road bond or clay soil will also help repel water in the same way.

Taller stones will need to be set in the ground deeply to secure them. Typically, one-third to one-half of a stone is set in the ground, depending on its shape. These stones will need to be set in what's called a *socket*. This is a hole in the ground large enough to accept the base of the stone and then some. If a stone is wider at the base than in the mid-section or top, the socket can be fairly shallow. If the base is narrow, you'll need a deeper socket. Once the stone is set in the hole, it needs to be plumbed or stood up straight by sighting with the naked eye. Or if the stone has a couple of flat vertical sides, a level can be used. With the stone standing straight, the socket around the base of the stone should be packed with smaller wedge-

shaped stones proportional to the standing stone. A thorough job of packing around the base of the stone is critical.

This large granite flake represents the north stone in a stone circle built by Clyde Hollifield. The 2-ton (1.9 t) stone measures 11 feet (3.3 m) in length. Only 7 feet (2.1 m) of the stone stands above ground.

One-third of this boulder is anchored into a berm.

SETTING A BOULDER IN A SOCKET

Sockets for stones lifted mechanically into the air can be relatively the size of the stone's lower third that will occupy the socket. Really large stones will require heavy equipment to hoist them, while smaller stones can be set with the help of a tripod (see page 129) or log rollers (see page 27). The socket for a boulder being rolled with logs will need to be much larger than the base of the stone to accommodate the angle at which the stone will lean into the hole.

When lifting a boulder with heavy machinery, consider using what's called a **megalithic hitch** (figure 2). This hitch is particularly useful when trying to lift the stone straight up in the air without any tilt to it, which means you can set the stone directly into its socket. This hitch won't work with stones that taper dramatically from bottom to top; it's best if the stone has a more cubed and oblong shape. All you need is a good length of chain with hooks at both ends that are capable of clamping onto a link anywhere along the chain's length.

Hold the first hook against one side of the stone down one-quarter of the stone's length from the top. Wrap the chain horizontally around the stone once and fasten it to hook #1, creating the lower loop. Make the loop as tight as possible.

Pull upward on the remaining chain, keeping tension at all times, and fasten the second hook to a link on the opposite side of the stone, directly in line with the first hook to create the upper loop. You'll need a separate chain and hook to attach the upper loop to whatever will be lifting the stone. As the stone is

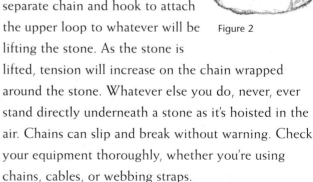

Figure 2

lifted, tension will increase on the chain wrapped around the stone. Whatever else you do, never, ever stand directly underneath a stone as it's hoisted in the air. Chains can slip and break without warning. Check your equipment thoroughly, whether you're using chains, cables, or webbing straps.

A large boulder is elevated above its socket on a log ramp. Each timber is hammered away while ropes and chains are used to pull the support timber, allowing the boulder to fall into the socket.

Standing Stones and Stone Circles

"The future is not to be found in the past. Yet, we know that the uppermost branch is fed by the deepest root. Ninety-five percent of our history as humans cannot be ignored. 'Written' by scavengers, hunters, gatherers, and early agriculturists, the story of the Stone Age is our story. Primitive technology is a way into that story. We are drawn to it as to a fire...and, there we find the others."

—Steve Watts, director of the Arboriginal Studies Program, Schiele Museum of Natural History, Gastonia, North Carolina

This section offers a glimpse into the megalithic phenomenon, both ancient and current. Megalithic is a Greek term meaning *mega* (great) and *lithos* (a rock or stone). Our Stone Age ancestors some 9,000 years ago began erecting mysterious groupings of stones that continue to mystify us.

An impressive number of sacred sites made up of a single standing stone (*menhirs*) and stone circles are located throughout Ireland and the British Isles. Elsewhere around the world, sites similar in structure and

Thor's Gate at Columcille Megalithic Park is created with two 15-ton (13.5 t) boulders and a 30-ton (27 t) lintel stone.

STONEHENGE

PERHAPS THE MOST FAMOUS STONE CIRCLE in the world is Stonehenge, located on the Salisbury Plain in England. The large standing stones of Stonehenge, called *sarcen stones*, were quarried and hand hewn almost 20 miles (32 km) away from where they now stand. Some of the larger monoliths weigh 45 tons (41 t) and stand in a circle approximately 97 feet (29 m) in diameter.

Neolithic tribes of the Stone Age built stone circles as gathering places for seasonal celebrations and ceremonies. As hunter-gatherers, and later as agrarian societies, these people lived close to the land and in complete awe of the starry heavens and the forces of nature that came thundering from the sky. With this relationship to the natural world and stone all around, it's understandable that stone would be the material of choice to create their temples honoring the earth and sky.

There was much symbolism involved in building these circular structures—setting stones to mark the four cardinal directions and solar and lunar points of alignment that signified important dates, such as the summer and winter solstices. Steeped in mythology and history, these circles evoke many mysteries and theories of exactly how and why they were built. With no written history, however, we're left to speculate exactly how these stone circles came to be.

Stonehenge is usually considered the crown jewel and the culmination of skills required in building stone circles. Unlike any other stone circle, the standing stones that formed Stonehenge were capped with connecting lentil stones. Mortises and tenons (typical in woodwork) were used to secure the lentils to one another and to the upright stones. It took 30 upright stones and 30 lintel stones to complete the outside circle.

A stone circle at Columcille.

appearance appear in Mexico, Brittany, and Sweden. There are also the equally impressive medicine wheels constructed by the North American Indians throughout the Northern Plains.

Why were these megalithic stones moved, and how, with Stone Age technology, were they stood upright? In our modern age, why are people still fascinated with the ancient stones and even today continue to build these stone circles?

It would be unrealistic to try to cover the ancient art and modern versions of standing stones in just this one section. I've combined my own experience in moving large stones for landscaping purposes with Rob Roy's insights and expertise in building stone circles. Rob Roy is one of the leaders in a revival of megalithic stone circle building going on today. His

latest book, *Stone Circles: A Modern Builders Guide to the Megalithic Revival* (Chelsea Green, 1999) is the best I've seen yet to combine historical, mythological, and modern information on building stone circles. It encompasses Rob's 20-year passion for visiting the ancient sites and building stone circles. I can't bestow more praise upon his book, and I thank him for sharing his experiences and wisdom.

BUILDING A STONE CIRCLE

There are a couple of different ways to approach designing a stone circle. One is simply to look at the aesthetics and sculptural qualities of how the stones work together within your landscape. The second method uses mathematical reasoning and alignments with the sun, moon, and stars. The original stone circles

Menanen, the largest "menhir" at Columcille Megalithic Park, weighs 35 tons (31.5 t) and stands 18 feet (5.4 m) tall with one-third of its height sunk into the ground. The shifting light on its heavily textured surface changes the mood of the setting throughout the day.

were designed with certain stones marking the four cardinal directions, or a particular alignment with the sun at solstice, marking the longest or shortest days of the year, along with other important dates. This method of designing will require more research of stone circles and your particular site.

SITE PREPARATION

Take some time to plan your circle. Taking as long as a year to plan it will give you plenty of time to gather the stones and to get familiar with your site. The stones you use should be in proportion with the site you choose. If you have a small space in the backyard, you'll want to go with smaller stones. If your site is open, as in a big field, the stones and diameter of the circle can be quite large. Keep in mind that once the stones are set, you want to be able to comfortably walk around the stones.

When choosing a site for your stone circle, be sure it has good drainage. This is critical, particularly in colder climates, because of frost heaving that could topple the stones. In extremely wet climates, the stones are likely to sink over time. It's possible to improve a low-lying site that has poor drainage by building the area up with layers of soil or road bond. The soil should be added in layers, 6 inches (15.2 cm) at a time and thoroughly compacted from one layer to the next.

THE STONES

Long, narrow stones are the easiest to handle and the most impressive for size-to-weight ratio. The proportions of the stone should be similar from one stone to the next, while the shapes, colors, and textures can dif-

Darin Roy, left, supervises installation of a stone commemorating his thirteenth birthday at Earthwood Building School in West Chazy, New York. The boys backfill and jam the socket with packing stones and soil.

This rippled sandstone from an ancient sea bottom stands just over 3 feet (1 m) above ground and weighs about 200 pounds (91 kg).

fer considerably. Stones that are extremely round are less impressive for their size and are harder to handle. Avoid soft stones and ones that have multiple vertical cracks and fissures. They're likely to fall apart during the moving and won't stand up to the weather for long. Catalog the stones by shape, size, approximate weight, and any outstanding characteristics. This information will be helpful in designing and setting the circle.

DESIGNS

A circle is the easiest and most common figure to work with but not the only one to be considered. Many of the ancient standing stones were placed in elliptical or egg shapes; flattened circles and even rectangles have been recorded. With a circle, you simply decide where you want the center to be and drive a wooden stake

there in the ground. Drive a nail partway into the top of the stake and hook your tape measure there. Draw the tape out half the distance of the circle's diameter, marking the radius. With the tape pulled taut, walk clockwise, which is "with the sun." The ancients avoided counterclockwise movements and called it "widdershins." It was considered back luck. Mark off the circle with pebbles, sand, cornmeal, or by scoring a line in the soil. Now you're ready to set the stones.

At this point you may have a pretty good idea of why you're building a stone circle. It may just be the challenge and thrill of standing the stones or that, aesthetically, a stone circle in the landscape appeals to you. The stillness of the stones brings grounding energy to the circle, creating a dynamic space of earth and sky.

A mowed path leads to a grassy knoll and The Merry Maidens stone circle near St. Buryan, Cornwall in England.

JAPANESE GARDENSCAPING

Duckweed lines the tranquil spillway pond and stone-lined stream bed that runs beneath an arched wooden bridge at The Horticulture Center of the Pacific in Victoria on Vancouver Island, British Columbia.

PUBLIC AND PRIVATE GARDENS, reflecting the temperate landscape of Japan, date back to the seventh century. These gardens have been influenced by the Chinese Buddhist aesthetic as well as by Japan's Shinto religion, and these idealized landscapes continue to evolve due to a culture that embraces an artful and unique interpretation of the natural world.

Japanese gardens symbolize the whole of nature on a microscopic scale. Harmony is created in the garden by blending materials that are easy on the eyes and inviting to the soul. A dry creek bed lined with waterworn stones could resemble a flowing river. Heavily pruned boxwoods and azaleas may imitate floating clouds, while a single moss- and fern-covered stone, set in the middle of a pond, might represent an island.

Masashi "Mike" Oshita

The projects and design information presented here convey the essence of Japanese gardening and its influences within a landscape.

Collaborating with me on this section is Masashi "Mike" Oshita, a Japanese master gardener. Mike's experience in gardening started at the age of 13, while working with his uncle, Kazuo Maeha, in Hiroshima, Japan. He later

In this modern Zen garden at the Tho-fu-ku-Ji Temple in Kyoto, Japan, boulders resembling coastal islands are set in a bed of raked gravel. Moss-covered mounds in the background echo the island shapes.

In Robin Hopper and Judi Dyelle's garden in Vancouver Island, British Columbia, rounded stones stabilize a slight slope into the pond, while a stone path leads up to one end of the bridge.

studied in Kyushu and in the traditional gardens of Kyoto. He's lived in the United States for the past 18 years and has been able to cross the cultural gap while remaining rooted in his native culture and heritage. Mike designs, builds, and maintains gardens through his business, Japanese Garden Services, located in Asheville, North Carolina.

I'll present a basic understanding of what a Japanese garden is and then, because this book is about stone, I'll focus primarily on using stones with their natural shapes, as well as carved stone features used in traditional and contemporary Japanese gardening. You don't have to create a full garden in order to enjoy one or more of the elements described here. Even one element is enough to change the focus of any garden space.

Garden Considerations

When you're creating a Japanese-style garden, a comprehensive understanding of the garden's proposed site is important. You'll need to consider your soil's pH, plants, climate zones, the slope of the land, tree inventory, outcroppings of stone and ravines, annual rainfall, the path of the sun, and the direction of prevailing winds.

For instance, a temperate climate allows for a wide selection of moisture-loving plants, such as bamboo, mosses, and ferns. In an arid desert setting where xeroscaping is practiced, the minimalist design of a traditional Zen garden, using stone groupings, gravel, and coarse sand, would seem appropriate.

Integrating a Japanese garden design with Western architecture and Western landscape practices can be a challenge, requiring careful planning. Stone, gravel, and sand complement the simple, clean lines of Japanese architecture and the traditional use of natural building materials. Porches, decks, walkways, and wooden fences extend the lines of a house outward, making interesting design elements with which to work. Components of the natural landscape, such as boulders and mature trees, and existing garden features, such as ponds, stone fences, and hedges can be successfully integrated with elements of a Japanese garden to create a provocative and intimate space.

DESIGN OPTIONS

The garden design shown below successfully combines several Japanese gardening styles. A dry creek bed of gravel and stone suggests the presence of water as it journeys from a distant mountaintop to a small pond. The organic shape of the pond is repeated in the outline of a pebbled path and then again with the semicircle created by large viewing stones. The path is connected by a stone bridge and draws you out into the garden's center. Stone lanterns offer visual interest—some are obscured by trees, while others stand in the open, accompanied by prominent viewing stones.

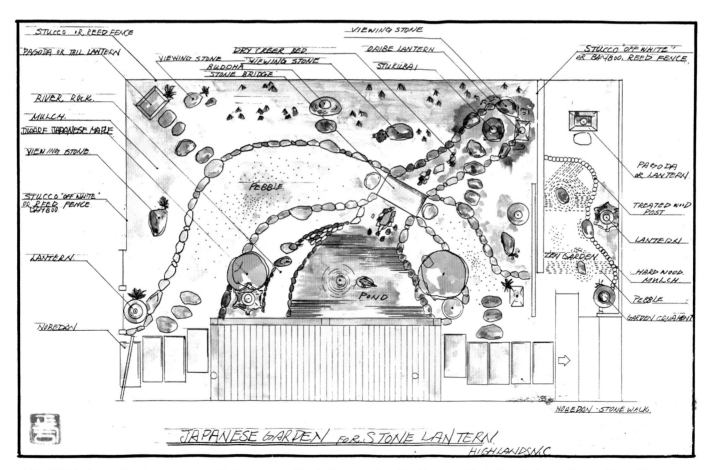

Mike Oshita's drawing for a Japanese garden illustrates many of the features mentioned in this section. To the far right is a small, fenced-in traditional Zen garden.

Stone in the Garden

Since before recorded history, stone has been highly revered by Japanese culture, many believing that spirits, referred to as *kami*, inhabit the rocks. This is particularly true of unusually shaped and weathered stones. When placed properly, stones not only bring structure and definition to the garden, but also, some believe, harmony and good fortune. The still water in a stone basin mirroring the sky above or moss clinging to the side of a stone represent calming yin energy. A group of stones rising out of a sea of gravel evokes the masculine yang energy.

STONE GROUPINGS

The proper placement of a stone in the traditional Japanese garden is studied at great length, with the search of each stone's inherent nature being part of the gardener's duty in determining its best placement. Often there is something about a stone's shape that suggests how to place it. Stones should blend effortlessly with the subtle color scheme in your garden. Groupings of stone bring a continuing sense of balance and harmony to a garden. Whether covered with snow, the transparent sheen of a summer rain, or the delicate petals of fallen tree blossoms, your stones' appearance will alter with the seasons.

Figure 3

In the Gentling Garden in Asheville, North Carolina, standing stones are set in deep sockets, and small boulders are placed in a low berm of road bond and soil. Gravel mulch surrounds low-growing boxwoods, azaleas, thyme, and Japanese mondo grass.

PLACEMENT DESIGNS

Odd numbers of stones are typical for stone groupings. Each grouping is often broken into subgroups of twos and threes, while mixing the heights and shapes of the stones create a pleasing visual combination. Three stones are used in the classic stone grouping, representing heaven, earth, and humankind. The central and largest stone represents heaven; the middle stone, earth; and the smallest one, humankind (figure 3).

One way to add visual interest when two or three stones are set together is to mound soil around the least visible side of the grouping, creating a slight berm for additional planting pockets.

Stones grouped together should have similar characteristics, especially color and surface texture. If you're selecting them from a natural setting, choose stones from the same general area or from the same pile at a stone yard. The size of the stones you choose should be in scale with the area where they're being placed. In extremely small spaces, large boulders can be overpowering, while in a large open area, small stones would appear insignificant.

SETTING STONES

In order to achieve an authentic and stable look, as much as one-third of a stone is buried, revealing only the most interesting features. At the very least, enough of the stone needs to be set in the ground so that it won't move or fall over. Gravel, moss, and low ground covering plants placed at a stone's base will help ground the stone visually. If you're using boulders that will require the use of heavy equipment, see page 149.

DECORATIVE VIEWING STONES

Viewing stones are single stones with enough visual interest to be set alone. These are some of the larger boulders in the garden, and they work well for filling in gaps between other garden features. A stone's most interesting focal point should be prominent for viewing from a path or deck.

Stone Features

Stone garden features carved from granite are expensive but a worthwhile investment. True stone features carved from granite will last many lifetimes. Garden features cast in concrete are close in resemblance, but with near inspection, it's easy to tell the difference. You can also carve your own features if you have the time and the skill. Since granite is a difficult stone to carve, you may want to try working with something softer, such as limestone.

STONE LANTERNS

Stone lanterns were originally used as prayer lamps at Buddhist temples. They were later introduced to Japanese gardens by tea masters, who used lanterns to light the stone water basins and garden paths leading to the teahouse. Lanterns placed in contemporary gardens are logically placed where paths intersect or near an interesting feature to be viewed, such as a bridge or an edge of a pond.

This low snow-viewing lantern is beautifully framed by the balanced grouping of weathered boulders.

There are many styles of Japanese lanterns. Here are a few basic designs: *Yukimi-gata*, or the snow-viewing lantern, sits close to the ground and works well in smaller intimate spaces.

Snow-viewing lantern

Tachi-gata lantern

Kasuga and *Tachi-gata* lanterns are tall with precise, ornate, and highly stylized features. The lantern consists of six separate parts: pedestal, shaft, mid-stage, light compartment, roof, and decorative finial or simple cap. *Orbie* lanterns are small and simple light features suitable for more intimate spaces.

Setting Lanterns

Larger lanterns that sit on a pedestal stone will need a foundation stone. A foundation stone should be at least 3 inches (7.6 cm) thick, with an even surface area that's twice as big as the base of the lantern's pedestal. Dig a shallow hole similar to the shape of the foundation stone and allow for a couple inches of packed gravel beneath it. After packing the gravel with a tamper, set the stone so its surface is just above ground level and pack soil around the sides.

The *Yukimi-gata*, will have two to four arching legs that will need to be leveled. Lanterns of this sort can be set directly on the ground or placed higher on top of a larger decorative viewing stone or natural rock outcropping.

Orbie-style lanterns have a supporting shaft with a flat bottom. If it's a small lantern with a short shaft, it may sit directly on the ground or on a flat base rock. Lanterns with a longer shaft may be sunk in a shallow hole with small stones packed around the shaft to secure it.

Pagodas

Set high on a slope, the stone tower or pagoda appears as a distant mountain shrine. When placed close to a pond's edge, its reflection is seen in the water's still surface, framed by blue sky and lily pads. Stone towers reaching toward the sky evoke a spiritual tone. Towers always have an odd number of individual tiers, with sides that are most often square. The stone tower you choose should be in proportion to the space it's going to occupy. The taller

A five-tiered pagoda

ones can reach heights of more than 15 feet (4.5 m).

Setting a Stone Tower

A stone tower will either have a solid base or four legs supporting it. Either way, it should have a foundation stone for extra support. Measure the tower's base, or the distance between the legs, and choose a stone with a surface area twice as large as your measurement. For larger towers, choose a foundation stone 6 inches (15.2 cm) thick, and set it according to the instructions for the larger stone lanterns.

TSUKUBAI OR WATER BASIN

The sight and sound of water in the garden are alluring to anyone close by. Symbolic of purity, the stone water basin is one way to bring the basic element of water into a garden. Traditionally associated with the Japanese tea ceremony, the *Tsukubai*, or stone water basin,

A Tsukubai (water basin) in its traditional setting

has its origins in the Shinto shrines of the mountains of Japan. Basins carved out of stone may be round, square, or rectangular. The hollowed-out center of the basin is filled with water from a pitcher or the overflow of a mountain spring, and a bamboo or wooden ladle is dipped into it to retrieve water. See page 141 for instructions on carving out your own basin.

In sixteenth-century Japan, it was customary for those attending the tea ceremony to wash their mouth and hands at the Tsukubai as an act of purification before entering the teahouse. Stone basins were set low to the ground, causing everyone, no matter what their social standing, to humble themselves by bending down close to the earth.

In a contemporary garden, the water basin is often used as a decorative feature that provides the soothing sound and enlivening sight of water. To keep the water in the basin fresh, replenish it daily either manually or with the help of a recirculating pump. When setting a water basin, make sure it has a visual landscape element to back up to, such as a house or garden wall, a rock ledge, or grouping of stones. It's customary and practical to place a stone lantern close by, providing a strong vertical element to the setting. Consider positioning the basin some distance away from other water features in the garden so these landscape elements won't be competing with one another.

Filling Your Basin

A stone water basin that's filled by hauling water to it or having a hose close by is the simplest way to maintain this feature. If the water basin is set in a shady area, the water will need to be topped off once a week, and more often if it's set in the sun. If the basin is left unattended for long periods, the water will evaporate or become stagnant, losing some of its visual appeal. To keep the water clean, occasionally scrub the basin's

A Shizen (natural style) water basin

interior with a mild solution of bleach and water. Any moss or coloration on the outside of the basin should be left as is if a weathered patina is desired.

To set up a slight trickle of water into the basin, run a garden hose to a *ka ke hi*, which is a bamboo post and spout used to direct the flow of water into the basin. To set up a source for water, a basic understanding of plumbing connections is necessary.

Each section of bamboo is marked on the outside by a ring; corresponding to the ring on the inside is a paper-thin layer that will need to be reamed out before you can run a hose through the bamboo.

A recirculating pump is necessary to keep the water flowing, which creates further audible and visual interest. Installing a pump requires electricity, a constant source of water, and a catch basin for the pump to sit in. Further instructions are available when you purchase your pump.

CATCH BASIN

To create a catch basin for the overflow from the stone basin, dig a hole 1 foot deep (.3 m) and wide enough to accommodate a water basin that's at least half as big as the stone basin. The hole will need to be wide enough for 6 to 8 inches (15.2 to 20.3 cm) of room all

the way around the base rock. Place a 2-inch (5.1 cm) layer of sand in the bottom of the hole in which to settle the base rock. Line the hole with a piece of pond liner, allowing it to overlap the rim of hole. Set the base stone, one without sharp edges, on top of the liner. Use the depth of the base stone to determine the overall height of the water basin.

Set a small pump (ones used for a large fish tank will do) in the bottom of the catch basin. Consult with an electrician for setting up a permanent power source close by, though an extension cord will do for a temporary electrical supply. Protect the cords from moisture. Run the flexible recirculating line from the pump through a piece of black plastic pipe that's slightly larger than the line coming off the pump. Run the plastic pipe with the line inside it up toward the top of the catch basin. This plastic pipe will help protect the line from being crushed by the stones in the catch basin.

Line the area around the pump with rounded stones slightly larger than the pump, then place a flat cover stone over the pump. Continue filling the catch basin with rounded stones of various sizes, using them to hide the black pipe as well. Bury the rest of the recirculating line in a sleeve of black pipe run around to the backside of the stone basin.

Tsukubai: Final Details

Place a single stepping stone in front of the catch basin. This stone can overlap the outside edge of the catch basin and rest on top of the liner's edge. Traditionally the Tsukubai had one prominent flat top stone on each side. One would be slightly higher than the other—the higher one used to hold an oil lamp or candle, while the other stone was where a bowl of warm water was placed for guests to wash their hands in colder weather. Visually these two stones help to anchor the basin and balance the overall composition.

STEPPING STONES

Stepping stones in a Japanese garden are a prominent element. On average, 3 to 4 inches (7.6 to 10.2 cm) of a stepping stone sits aboveground with the remaining thickness set into the earth. Bare earth and ground covers of gravel, coarse sand, moss, or pine needles contrast against the stones, as the different paths guide garden visitors through the landscape.

The distance between individual stepping stones determines the pace one keeps when walking a path. Stepping stones in a Japanese garden are set in groups of two and three. They're set close together to slow the pace when garden features are in view. Stones are also deliberately laid out in offset patterns that cause a person to step slowly, keeping them mindful of the beauty and tranquillity that surround them in the garden.

Arranging the stepping stones in a pleasing and harmonious manner takes time.

Set in a zigzag pattern, these stepping stones take a meandering route across a pond at the Heian Jingu Shinto Shrine in Kyoto, Japan.

Stepping stones lead to a Tsukubi in a tea garden.

Avoid setting stones in a straight line; this would be out of sync with the rest of the garden. Suitable for the Japanese garden are stepping stone patterns that emulate nature, such as wide and shallow curves, zigzag formations, or a V-shape resembling a flock of geese.

Stone paths should be set in place after large viewing stones, stone groupings, and features such as basins and lanterns have been added. Stepping stones with the largest surface area should be set first and used in prominent spots: a pivot stone at intersecting paths, next to a water basin, by a lantern or a pond's edge. Place the most foot-friendly surface of a stone on top and the irregular surface in the ground.

Figure 4

Most often, the gap between two stones will be formed where two parallel edges of the stones line up. If one stone has a concave edge, the next one should have a convex edge. Never set two stones together with pointed edges facing one another. A harmonious arrangement of stone shapes and their alignment to one another are desirable.

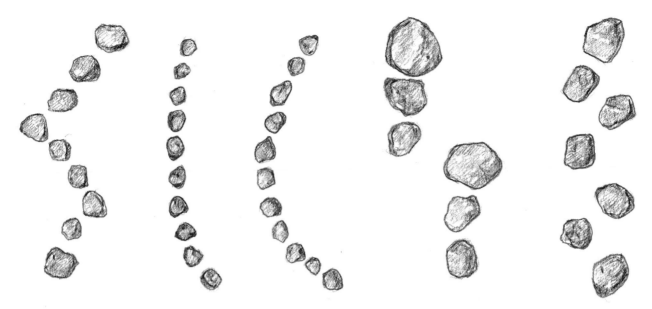

Figure 5: A variety of stepping-stone designs, from left to right: Flying Geese, Slow Curve, Sharp Curve, Three and Three, and Bird Stepping on Beach

Moving Stones

Move stepping stones with a hand truck, ball cart, or wheelbarrow. A tripod with a chain hoist may be helpful for setting larger stones (see page 149). Often, stones with a large surface area can be stood on their edge and walked into place by turning the stones like a wheel. This is usually easier with two people. Once a stone is lying where it will be set, use a digging bar to adjust the rock exactly where you want it. This is done by thrusting the pointed end of the bar in the ground beneath the edge of the stone, then bumping the stone with the bar to move it in small increments.

Placing Stepping Stones

Use a tape measure to check the thickness of the stone you're about to set. With a shovel and mattock, dig an area that's wide and deep enough to accommodate the base of the stone while leaving about 3 to 4 inches (7.6 to 10.2 cm) above ground. Use a digging bar to pry underneath and set wedge stones, if necessary, as you level the stone by eye or with a 2-foot (.6 m) level. Pack around the stones with soil or pea gravel once you're satisfied with the path's overall layout.

STONE PAVEMENT

A paved stone pathway is appropriate for long, straight paths, 2½ to 3 feet (.75 to .9 m) wide, in open spaces of a garden. Dry-laid and mortared paving techniques can be used for this type of stone placement, with a wide variety of patterns to choose from. Set the paving several inches aboveground, like the stepping stones, or just out of the ground, depending on the desired look. Groups of stepping stones can be used to break up long runs of paving and are necessary when making turns in a path. For a consistent look, set the longest and straightest edge of each stone to the outside of the path, creating a substantial frame in which to set smaller stones. Large, unusually shaped stones can be set so they protrude beyond the outside edge along the length of the path.

Light snow falls on the diamond-patterned path of hand-hewn granite stepping stones which leads to Ginkaku-Ji (The Silver Pavilion Temple) in Kyoto, Japan.

ACKNOWLEDGMENTS

I'd like to thank friends, old and new, for contributing many beautiful and extraordinary photographs to this book:

David Hildebrand: half title; title page; pages 6, 7 BR, 41, 132, and 133 T

Mike Oshita: pages 133 B, 163, 168, 169, 170, 171, 172, and 174

Bob Tiller: pages 13 TL, 16 T, 30, 77, and 104

Jane Wooley: pages 43, 49, 50, 52, and 53

Rob Roy pages 27, 130, 131, and 160

Darin Roy: page 155

Jeff Ashton: pages 13 BR, 42, 46, and 49

Frederica Lashley: pages 57, 58 B, 59, 60, and 119

Sally Broughton pages 157 and 161

Bill Laity: pages 120 and 121 L

Rick Woods (Earth Light Photography) pages 4 and 51

Artisans and the pages their work appears on:

Stone carvers:

TOM JACKSON
Dellrose Artisans
POB 130
Ardmore, TN 38449
1-800-732-4812
Pages 11, 134, and 135

JIM MORRIS
5343 Tollgate Rd.
Pipersville, PA 18947
(215) 297-5487
Jamore@ hotmail.com
Pages 66 T, 70, and 139

VERENA SCHWIPPERT
Sculptures and Paintings
245 West 4th Street
Arlington, WA 98223
(360) 435-8849
Page 136

CHRIS BERTI
106 West Washington St.
Urbana, IL 61801
(217) 384-9010
Page 137

Stonemasons:

FREDERICA (FRED) LASHLEY
The Unturned Stone
3364 Crooked Creek Rd.
Mars Hill, NC 28754

(828) 689-9116
Pages 57, 59

JOE ROBERTS
Stoneweavers
Stonescaping
65 Ballard Branch Rd.
Weaverville, NC 28787
(828) 645-4834
Page 26

JIM MACMILLAN
Fine Stone Work
Boone, NC 28607
(828) 262-0449
Page 109

JEFF NELSON
Stoneworks Masonry
P.O. Box 452
Ridgecrest, NC 28770
(828) 669-4818
Pages 37, 145

DAVID REED
The Circle of Stone
P.O. Box 1293
Asheville, NC 28802
www.stonescaping.com
davidpreed@mindspring.com
Pages 55, 69, 72, 76, 83, 85, 91, 95, 99, and 105

Landscape designers:

MIKE OSHITA
Japanese Garden Service
P.O. Box 16934
Asheville, NC 28816
(828) 626-2300
Page 165

WILLIAM R. LAITY LANDSCAPE COMPANY
180 Blackberry Inn Rd.
Weaverville, NC 28787
(828) 645-6538
Pages 96, 97, and 122

Stone suppliers featured in the book:

NORTHWEST LANDSCAPE & STONE SUPPLY
5883 Byrne Rd.
Burnaby, B. C. V5J3J1
(604) 435-4842 or 14904
Smokey Point Boulevard
Marysville, WA 98270
(360) 651-2144
www.huckleberrystone.com

DELAWARE QUARRIES, INC.
Route 32
Lumberville, PA 18933
(215) 297-5647

J.R. STONE SALES INC.
171 Lyman St.
Asheville, NC 28802
(828) 285-9288

STILLS STONE COMPANY
1504 Charlotte Hwy.
Fairview, NC 28730
(828) 628-3455

SILVARA STONE COMPANY
309 County Seat Rd.
Crossville, TN
(931) 484-6653

MARENAKOS ROCK CENTER
30250 S.E. High Point Way
Issaquah, WA 98027
(206) 392-3313

Stone organizations

DRY STONE CONSERVANCY, INC.
1065 Dove Run Road, Suite 6
Lexington, KY 40502
(859) 266-4807
www.DryStoneUSA.org

STONE FOUNDATION
116 Lovato Lane,
Santa Fe, NM 87505
(505) 989-4644
www.stonefoundation.org

THE DRY STONE WALLING ASSOCIATION OF GREAT BRITAIN
PO Box 8615, Sutton Coldfield B75 7HQ
0121-378-0493
www.dswa.org.uk

COLUMCILLE MEGALITHIC PARK
2155 Fox Gap Road
Bangor, PA 18013
(610) 588-1174
www.columcille.org

EARTHWOOD BUILDING SCHOOL
Rob and Jaki Roy
366 Murtagh Hill Rd.
West Chazy, NY 12992
(518) 493-7744
www.bigstones.com

HORTICULTURE CENTER OF THE PACIFIC
505 Quayle Rd.
Victoria, B.C. V9E2J7
(250) 479-616

Location photography:

Nelson and Deborah Woodard, Delaware Township, NJ
Greg Olson and Rosalind Willis, Weaverville, NC
Winterberry Farm,

Haywood County, NC
Evan Moquah and Jackie Taylor, Turtle Run Farm, Hot Springs, NC
Martin and Barbara Webster, Starforest Quilts, Burnsville, NC
Richard and Ginger Lang, Crabtree, NC
Marge and Mac Cates, Linville, NC
Sid and Emily Heilbraun, Asheville, NC
Clyde and Adrienne Hollifield, Black Mountain, NC
Darryl D. Nabors D.D.S., Clyde, NC
Mike and Polly Hutchinson, Casey Farm, Saunders Town, RI
Dave and Elaine Whitehead, North Saanich, Vancouver Island, BC
The garden of Robin Hopper and Judi Dyelle
@Chosin Pottery Inc. 4283 Metchosin Road
Victoria, Vancouver Island, B.C. Canada
(250) 274-2676
The North Carolina Arboretum Society, 100 Frederick Law Olmsted Way, Asheville, NC 28806

Special thanks to:

Jane Wooley of the Dry Stone Conservancy, Dr. Lara Setti, Clyde Hollifield, Joe Roberts, Evan Moquah, Chip Smith, Anthony Neal, Marjorie Vestal, Tom Boyd, Iris Photographics, Michael Greenfield, Don Fraser, Paul Moore, Amy Burkett, Sam Taylor, Nancy Reed, Paul Arnold, and Andrea Latier

My thanks to Sterling Publishing, Inc. and Carol Taylor, publishing director of Lark Books, for the opportunity to author *The Art and Craft of Stonework;* the great staff at Lark Books, with special thanks to my editor Joe Rhatigan for bringing a genuine sense of order and understanding to a mountain of text; and thank you Celia Naranjo, for adding your splendid sense of aesthetic to the book's pages.

INDEX